OVERVIEW

Overview
  Preparing a Business Plan
There are four main benefits of preparing a business plan. It helps you clarify what developments your business should focus on. It also gives you a framework within which to develop your business strategies. It acts as a benchmark against which actual performance can be measured, and it gives you influence over the direction your business or department takes.

Business plans differ from strategic plans. Business plans are created by start-ups and established businesses alike. However, business plans created by the latter are usually exclusively for internal use.

Your business plan should include four main elements. It should describe the opportunity it addresses and then the solution you've come up with. It should then detail the plan's execution, and finally it should include the desired outcomes of the plan. Once you've considered each element, you can create a narrative from them.

Preparation is of great importance when developing a business plan. Prepare for the development by discussing, thinking, researching, and analyzing your business ideas.

There are six steps you should take when preparing to develop your business plan. The first of these is defining your mission. The second step is doing research to identify key issues related to your idea. The next step is establishing goals. Next, you need to identify strategies to achieve your goals. And finally, you'll assess resources and identify risks.

Your business plan will vary depending on its purpose. It typically comprises four major parts. These are the executive summary, the market opportunity, the implementation, and the contingencies. Complete each of these with your target audience in mind.

There are several guidelines to follow when creating an effective business plan. First, keep it short. Make sure to pay special attention to the executive summary. Next, tell a compelling story and make sure your plan fits the business need. Also, be realistic and specific. Finally, use a reader-friendly page layout and writing style.

Performing Key Analyses

A business plan will typically include an executive summary, information on market opportunities, the implementation details of the plan, and any necessary contingencies due to unexpected changes in market conditions.

Benefits to performing situational analyses include informing the future direction of your business plan, identifying resources and capabilities, and allowing you to explore any potential issues that may arise.

When conducting an internal analysis, there are four areas to consider: assessing market strategy, assessing resources, evaluating organizational and management strategy, and evaluating your organization's financial position.

An external analysis of a business environment includes careful consideration of political, economic, societal, and technological factors – otherwise known as a PEST analysis.

Scenario planning takes these important factors and examines how a business plan might change under different political, economic, societal, and technological circumstances.

A market analysis consists of identifying customer groups, inspecting the industry, and analyzing the competitors within that industry.

A SWOT analysis uses information from your internal and external analyses to define strategies to maximize competitive advantage. The internal analysis identifies strengths and weaknesses in your company's strategy, resources, and financial position. An external analysis will provide information on the political, economic, societal, and technological environment. It will also outline customer needs, competitors' capabilities, and industry trends.

Your SWOT will help find the best fit for your available resources and capabilities to match to your competitive environment. You'll derive a number of strategies that you can prioritize to your advantage when you draw up a business plan. Strategies include strength-opportunity strategies, weakness-opportunity strategies, strength-threat strategies, and weakness-threat strategies.

Preparing for Implementation

You should view the planning, implementation, and control phases of a business plan as part of a continuous strategic process. This should help you implement it successfully and achieve real benefits.

To coordinate the implementation of your business plan, you should follow a number of steps. First, develop action plans that outline the tasks that need to be completed. Next, ensure that implementation can be supported in your organization. Create a reporting system to help you monitor progress. Be sure you can control and modify your plans. And finally, assess the outcomes.

When implementing a business plan, the first step is to develop action plans. To create an action plan, first clarify the outcomes you want to achieve. For each outcome, list the activities necessary to achieve it. Then put the activities in order.

Next, assign responsibilities for completing each activity. Determine the resources you need to implement your plan. And determine the likely costs of implementing it. Finally, create a schedule showing the timelines involved.

To generate support for your action plan, you may need to reallocate resources, realign responsibilities, relate rewards to results, and review procedures and policies.

It's important to make sure your business plan can be measured and controlled. You can create a management reporting system to help you do this.

To create a reporting system, you need to define key performance indicators – and set parameters for each one. You also need to relate performance measures to employee behavior and use comparative data to identify trends. Finally, you need to structure report formats effectively.

If reports indicate that you're not achieving the expected results, you should react quickly and decisively to the situation by modifying your original plan. First, identify the problem areas in your plan. Next, pinpoint the probable cause of each problem. Then you can develop a corrective-action strategy. The final step is to implement and monitor the new strategy.

CHAPTER ONE
Preparing a Business Plan

The four key elements of a business plan
Business plan benefits

Planning for the future is crucial for any successful organization, and business plans play an important part in that process. Without a business plan, your organization or department could easily become directionless. Your business plan sets out how you'll navigate foreseeable and unforeseeable opportunities and challenges as you pursue your business ideas. Your plan should describe your objectives and how you'll achieve them in a coherent, consistent, and cohesive manner.

Consider this example of business planning. Phyllis is a manager in the Marketing Department of a clothing retailer. She's finishing a presentation on a new business plan she has been busy preparing. Phyllis is looking to Scott and Krista, her colleagues in the department, for their feedback before she presents the plan to senior management for approval.

Follow along as Phyllis talks to Scott and Krista.

Phyllis: So the plan gets us to focus on using targeted marketing to better effect. The goal being to grow sales by 10% over each of the next three years...And that's it really. What do you think?

Phyllis is formal but friendly.

Krista: Sounds good! I like the year-to-year target plans – clearly laid out. And the way you showed how they'll benefit the firm. But are you sure senior management will give it a green light?

Krista is concerned.

Phyllis: I'm hoping...a strong selling point is that they'll be able to consult the plan to check that we're doing what we said we would! Scott, what about you?

Phyllis is thoughtful.

Scott: I'm impressed. It addresses some of my concerns about this change of direction. You've got my support!

Scott is enthusiastic.

Reflect

Based on Phyllis's situation, what benefits do you think are derived from preparing a business plan?

Write down your response or enter it in a text file in your word-processor application (or in a text editor such as Notepad) and save it to your hard drive for later viewing.

You may have noted that preparing a business plan helps you clarify which developments your business or project should focus on. It gives you a logical framework within which to develop your business strategies over time. And while those strategies are unfolding, a plan acts as a benchmark against which actual performance can be measured. Finally, a plan is the key to giving you influence over the direction your business or department takes.

Question

Business plans can be used as benchmarks against which real progress may be measured.

Is this statement true or false?

Options:

1. True
2. False

Answer

Option 1: This statement is true. By mapping out what direction you want your organization to go in over a specified period of time, you are providing your organization with a benchmark against which to measure progress.

Option 2: This statement is not false. Business plans act as benchmarks against which actual progress in fulfilling the plan's goals can be measured.

Elements of business plans

How do strategic plans and business plans differ? Strategic plans are longer than business plans, the former covering a period of up to ten years with the latter covering one or two years. Strategic plans tend to focus on broad, high-level objectives, such as increasing sales by 20% over the next five years. Business plans, however, include concrete, short-term strategies and tactics, like launching a new product in the next quarter. Business plans should support an organization's broader strategic objectives.

When you think of business plans, you might think of start-up organizations in search of venture capital. However, that's not the only situation in which an organization may create a plan. Established organizations create business plans for their internal use rather than for outside investors or third parties.

Departmental managers within large organizations prepare business plans to gain approval and secure resources from senior management for department-specific developments. These plans may map out the development of new products, services, processes, or expansion into new markets. They might even detail plans for taking over rival firms or changing processes.

Your business plan should be consistent with your organization's objectives, strategic demands, and financial resources. If your plan is at odds with any of these, it reduces the chances it will be accepted by senior management.

There's a lot of preparation that needs to go into a business plan before it's presentable to an audience. You need to think about how you'll prepare your own business plan. You can do this by becoming familiar with and considering each of the elements that make up an effective business plan. Each element will flow from the previous one, so it's important to give each due consideration from the start.

Question

Which elements do you think a business plan includes?

Options:

1. A problem you plan to solve or an idea you want to implement
2. A description of the solution to a problem or the proposed idea
3. Results or projected financial outcomes
4. An organization's long-term strategic goals

5. Information for setting and monitoring an organization's long-term objectives

Answer

Option 1: This option is correct. A business plan typically starts with an executive summary that describes what the plan is proposing – for example, a solution to a problem or the introduction of a new idea.

Option 2: This option is correct. A business plan describes the solution or idea by explaining, for example, how a product or service works, how it solves the problem, its customer base, and its price and positioning.

Option 3: This option is correct. A business plan includes projected financial outcomes. In this part of the plan, you estimate what the results will be if your plan is followed.

Option 4: This option is incorrect. The long-term goals of the organization are included in the strategic plan. These goals do influence the business plan because it should align with any goals set at the organizational level.

Option 5: This option is incorrect. Information for setting and monitoring an organization's long-term objectives is typically found in the strategic plan. The plan acts as a tool for senior management and the board of directors to develop and direct a firm's long-term operations.

When you are creating a plan, there are four elements, or broad areas, you typically cover. First, you describe the opportunity or idea you're proposing, followed by the solution you've come up with – the second element. Third, the plan should detail the execution – that is, how your plan will actually be undertaken. Finally, the plan should describe the desired outcomes.

See each element to find out more information.

Opportunity

The opportunity element of your business plan describes the problem your plan will solve, or how a particular business idea will benefit your department and the organization. It goes on to describe who has the problem or who will benefit from the idea, what trends affect the problem or idea, and how much people will be willing to spend. This section is essentially an investigation of the market.

For example, the business plan of an athletic shoe retailer outlines a new sports trend that the retailer sees as an opportunity for growth.

Solution

The solution addresses the opportunity you've identified by describing the product or service you'll introduce, the change you're proposing, or whatever your idea may involve. Issues you'll address in this section include things like how the product or service works and how it solves a problem or provides a particular benefit, as well as its customer base, its price and positioning, and how it compares to competitors' offerings.

For example, a confectionary company includes the development of a range of sugar-free candy in its business plan. This is to meet the demands of health-conscious parents who seek lower-calorie treats for their children.

Execution

The execution element describes how you'll develop your idea – be it a product or service or something else – to bring it to market or get it successfully implemented. In this section, you would consider what resources you'll need to create and distribute your product. You'll also need to consider how you'll attain market share and preserve it. You should be clear about what might go wrong and how you'll mitigate problems.

For example, managers at an electronics company know that their plan to create a new cell phone and capture a good share of that market will require extensive coordination between the Product Development Department, the consumer research unit, and the Marketing Department.

Outcomes

The outcome element explains what you imagine the results will be if your plan is followed. You'll anticipate sales and revenue over the coming years and explain how you'll deal with changes in the market during that period.

For example, a nutritional supplement company projects a 30% increase in sales over the coming five years if its business plan is adopted.

Consider Stuart, the R&D manager of a software firm. He's looking for an opportunity. Having young children, he's increasingly drawn to technologies that help ease parents' fears and make children safer. Stuart talks to colleagues who have children and to parents outside of the firm to find out what they want in terms of software. He finds their biggest fear is that their children will interact with adult strangers online, so he decides to develop a business plan to address their fears.

Viewing this issue as an opportunity, he starts working on a solution. After further research and brainstorming with his team, he decides to create a social network specifically for children and young teenagers. This network will allow children to interact online in a safe environment.

Business Planning

With regard to the execution, Stuart believes his staff can complete the network in a short period of time and that parent-targeted advertising can become the primary revenue source. He includes an outline of a promotional campaign that will target parents of elementary school children.

Finally, Stuart describes the outcomes of his plan. He estimates usage and revenue for the coming years and includes provisions for updating the product as new competitors enter the market. Having considered and researched each of the elements, Stuart can now put his plan together and present it to senior management.

The four elements will help you organize your thoughts as you begin to prepare your business plan. Consider your opportunity, your solution, the execution, and the likely outcomes of your business plan.

Your final business plan will tie each of these elements together into a coherent narrative, which you can then use to persuade your audience of the value of your business ideas and plan.

Question

Match each example to the corresponding business plan element.

Options:

A. A detergent retailer's plan addresses complaints about cleaning product toxicity by proposing an environmentally-friendly product line

B. A furniture firm's plan includes a proposal for increased marketing that should lead to higher visibility in foreign markets

C. A toy company's plan begins by showing how a line of toys that promote physical activity are in demand among parents

D. A hardware firm plans to implement a new carpentry product by focusing on increased production

Targets:
1. Opportunity
2. Solution
3. Execution
4. Outcomes

Answer

The increasing popularity of toys that promote physical activity is an opportunity for the toy company.

The detergent retailer sees a solution to customer needs in stocking more environmentally-friendly products.

Increasing production is one means of execution of a business plan that focuses on implementing a new product.

Higher visibility in foreign markets is an outcome that a business plan may describe.

Activity - **Organizing Your Thoughts**

You can print this document, or recreate the table in a word processing or spreadsheet application and use it to complete this activity. Add your thoughts on each element of your business plan to the relevant section of the table.

Business plan element	Your thoughts on the element of the business plan
Opportunity	
Solution	
Execution	
Outcomes	

Steps in developing a business plan
Defining your mission

When creating a business plan, success largely depends on how much preparation you put in. The vast majority of the work in an effective business plan is typically done in the preparatory stages. By closely following preparatory steps, you're less likely to leave out anything important from your plan. And once you've done the groundwork, you should then find it easy to write your business plan and present it to its intended audience.

But what does preparation entail? You can start preparing to develop your business plan through discussion with your coworkers. Develop understanding and insights and work at activities that help generate ideas for the business. Be aware that planning is an ongoing process that includes extensive research and analysis. As your plan develops, you may have to revise parts of it, so allow for flexibility in your preparations.

There are many questions you'll need to address as you prepare your business plan. For example, is your plan consistent with and supportive of your business's overall strategy? Is it feasible? And what resources are needed to make it a reality?

Other questions you should ask relate to the likely impact your plan will have in terms of revenue growth and profitability. Will the plan require additional financing and have an impact on other departments within the business?

It's crucial that you anticipate and address any issues that decision makers in your organization may raise about your plan to ensure it gets the go-ahead.

Reflect

What steps do you think you'd take when preparing to develop your business plan?

Write down your response or enter it in a text file in your word-processor application (or in a text editor such as Notepad) and save it to your hard drive for later viewing.

There are six steps in the planning process for developing business plans, some of which you may have noted in your response. You first define your mission, and then you do the required research. After that, you establish the goals of your plan. Next, identify the strategies you'll use to meet those goals. You'll then assess resources. Finally, you'll identify risks associated with implementing your plan.

When starting to develop your business plan, you first define your mission or purpose. Organize your thoughts by considering the four business plan elements. Think about what opportunity you'll pursue – for example, the problem your plan addresses. Next, consider the solution – for example, a product or service you'll create to solve the problem. Then think about the execution – how you'll bring that product or service to market. Finally, contemplate the likely outcomes of your plan.

When defining the mission or purpose of your business plan, it's also important to know who your audience will be. Different types of audiences will focus on different aspects of the plan.

For example, if your business plan is for a department within a large organization, senior management might focus on its potential impact on the organization's competitiveness, revenue, or profitability. If your plan is intended to entice outside lenders or investors, they may focus on whether the plan can guarantee loans will be repaid or that there will be a good return on any investment.

While each audience will closely examine the sections that address their particular interests, they'll all be interested in the overall soundness of your plan.

For example, consider Ayana, the team leader in the Customer Service Department of a telecommunications firm. She commences her preparation by defining the purpose of the plan.

She believes more high-value customers can be retained if her department changes. Her solution is a new 24-hour customer support web site. She outlines how this will be implemented and suggests the outcomes will include higher customer retention and higher productivity in the department.

When defining the purpose of the plan, she makes sure its benefits will be clear to the senior managers who ultimately decide whether the plan is enacted. She decides her plan's mission is to improve the end-user experience for high-value customers, to preserve lucrative relationships.

Question

In what order should the steps in preparing to develop a business plan be taken?

Options:

A. Define your mission
B. Do research
C. Establish goals
D. Identify strategies to meet goals
E. Assess resources
F. Identify risks

Answer

Correct answer(s):

Define your mission is ranked the first step. Defining your mission is the first step you take when preparing to develop your business plan.

Do research is ranked the second step. You do research as the second step in preparing to develop your business plan.

Establish goals is ranked the third step. You establish goals as the third step in the process, directly after doing research.

Identify strategies to meet goals is ranked the fourth step. Identifying strategies to meet your plan's goals is the fourth step you take in the preparatory process.

Assess resources is ranked the fifth step. Assessing the resources available to you is the fifth step in preparing to develop a business plan.

Identify risks is ranked the sixth step. Identifying risks is the sixth and final step in the preparatory process for developing your business plan.

Doing research

The second step in preparing to develop your business plan is to do research. Initially, you should identify critical issues – for example, potential sources of internal funding and resource allocation. Next, ensure any ideas you have align with your organization's strategy. This may require reviewing key corporate documents and strategic plans. Then undertake situation, external, and gap analyses to ensure your plan is viable. And finally, consider the customer – how will this plan improve customer experience or satisfaction levels?

See each technique to find out more information.

Identify critical issues

Before delving deeply into sources of information, identify the most important issues your business plan will address. Consider things that may hinder you from moving forward if they're not addressed.

Ensure ideas align with strategy

As you research the ideas for your plan, make sure they align with your business's overall strategy and mission. A mission statement provides the overall vision from which organizational strategy and objectives are set. Including ideas that don't align with your organization's mission and strategy will only serve to undermine your business plan.

Undertake analyses

There are several types of analyses you can use while researching your plan. An internal analysis examines factors within your department or organization that may affect your idea and its successful implementation. This helps you gauge what resources will be available for your business plan.

An external analysis looks at your customers, competition, and market. This helps you decide how your business plan will be marketed and how it will deal with competitors.

And a gap analysis examines the difference between your department's current state and its desired state according to your plan. This helps identify the intended outcomes of your business plan.

Consider the customer

When considering your customers, you may review consumer information related to your industry. Considering what your customers want and need contributes toward you creating a plan that will benefit your entire organization.

For example, Karl is the R&D Department manager of an electronics company. He has defined his mission, which is to propose that his department start focusing on products for the tablet PC peripherals market. He undertakes research to help him decide what peripherals the department should concentrate on, bearing in mind that his ideas must fit with the company's overall strategy.

Karl considers the issues in developing peripherals for tablet PCs. Compatibility, security, and price are all significant areas of consideration. He also considers internal, external, and gap analyses. In terms of the internal analysis, he might examine what kind of similar products his company already produces or has plans to develop.

Externally, he might ask whether any of the company's direct competitors have launched similar products recently and if there's sufficient demand.

His gap analysis might focus on where the company is today compared to where it wants to be, and what needs to happen in order to reach its ultimate goals.

Finally, Karl examines consumer data that shows which models of tablet PC are popular sellers, and also highlights what types of peripherals the company's customers would want. He now has enough information to be able to continue on to the next preparatory step in developing his business plan.

Question

Match the examples to the corresponding steps in preparing to develop a business plan. Each step may have more than one match.

Options:

A. Martin, the head of marketing at a bicycle retailer, identifies what problem his business plan should address

B. Ted, an IT manager, makes sure his business ideas fit his investment firm's long-term strategy

C. Karen considers the execution and likely outcomes of a business plan that will help modernize the financial firm she works for

D. Rhonda, who works for a retail firm, does a situation analysis of the Finance Department as part of preparation for her business plan

Targets:

1. Define your mission
2. Do research

Answer

Identifying a problem or opportunity and considering execution and outcomes are ways of defining your mission.

Making sure business ideas align and doing situation and other analyses are ways of doing research for a business plan.

Establishing goals

Having completed the research for your business plan, you then establish your goals. This is the third step in the preparatory process for developing a business plan. By establishing goals, you're setting out what your plan will aim for. You're also laying out the parameters within which your plan will operate.

When establishing your goals, it's important to be realistic about what you can achieve in implementing your business plan.

Don't be overly optimistic about what your plan will achieve, as is often the case with projected sales or revenue increases. Similarly, don't underestimate what financial and other resources you require to make your plan a reality, as it'll be hard to seek additional resources when your plan has already commenced.

If you're working at a departmental level, consider whether your goals conflict with those of other departments' plans. When a conflict occurs, work to achieve a compromise that is to the satisfaction of all involved.

Peggy, the recruitment team leader at an energy company, is creating a business plan. After defining the plan's mission and doing a lot of research, she works on establishing the plan's goals. She aims to attract more top graduates from leading universities to the company.

When predicting the number of top tier graduates her plan will attract, she's careful to give a conservative estimate. She knows the company has significant competitors who are also vying for highly-skilled new workers. Part of the plan is dedicated to making the company a more attractive workplace for new recruits by offering better starting terms and more flexibility.

Peggy's also aware that her plan to attract top graduates may be at odds with the Finance Department's goal of lowering staff costs. With this in mind, she organizes a meeting with the Finance Department manager to come to an agreement on what salary and benefits the recruitment team may offer potential new staff members.

Question

Which examples illustrate the establishing goals step in preparing to develop a business plan?

Options:

1. Polly does a situation analysis of her department as part of preparations for a business plan

2. Glen knows his intention of increasing sales by 5% over the next year is within the sales team's abilities

3. Anna, the Production Department head at a design firm, makes sure the results she's looking for won't conflict with the other departments' goals

4. Luke spends time deciding what opportunity his business plan will address

Answer

Option 1: This option is incorrect. Situation, external, and gap analyses are all ways of doing research, the second step in preparing to develop a business plan.

Option 2: This option is correct. Being realistic about what you can achieve is an important part of establishing goals for your business plan.

Option 3: This option is correct. Considering whether goals conflict is an important factor in the establishing goals step.

Option 4: This option is incorrect. Considering the opportunity of a business plan is part of defining your mission, the first preparatory step.

Identifying strategies

Identifying the strategies you'll use to fulfill your goals is the fourth step you'll take when preparing to develop your business plan. Strategies comprise the pattern of purposes, policies, and actions you undertake to achieve your plan's goals. Think about what strategies might fit best with your organization and business goals.

The strategies you adopt to pursue your plan's goals should clearly link to your department or organization's environment. This is true even if they're implemented to alter that environment. Your strategies should also be suitable, feasible, and acceptable to all involved in the plan.

Consider Audrey, the design coordinator at a furniture company. She's preparing to develop a business plan. The plan's goals include modernizing the company's output by engaging with design schools and student designers. This will fulfill the plan's mission of increasing the company's relevance among young consumers.

When choosing which strategies to use to fulfill these goals, Audrey carefully considers the current work environment. Many staff members have worked there for a long time and she doesn't want to alienate them. So she picks a strategy that entails evolutionary change rather than a significant break with the past.

She decides that one way to bridge the gap between the younger designers and the staff is to hold a series of short coffee meetings. This is so the young designers and her established staff can get to know one another on a less formal basis before they actually start working together. To ensure this is actually feasible, she first checks that current staff members do not have any reservations about this approach.

Question

Which examples illustrate identifying strategies as part of preparing to develop a business plan?

Options:

1. Gloria chooses a dynamic strategy for her business plan that suits the frantic pace in her department

2. Liz checks whether staff members support her business strategy to use automation to increase productivity

3. Timothy reviews a lot of consumer data when preparing a business plan for the technical support hub of a computer manufacturer

4. Rebecca includes realistic projections for her company's growth in her business plan

Answer

Option 1: This option is correct. When identifying strategies to fulfill your plan's goals, you should make sure your strategy links to the work environment.

Option 2: This option is correct. When identifying strategies for your plan, you should make sure the strategies are suitable, feasible, and acceptable to all involved.

Option 3: This option is incorrect. Considering the customer is a key part of the doing research step in preparing for developing a business plan.

Option 4: This option is incorrect. Being realistic about what can be achieved is a component of the establishing goals step in preparing for developing a plan.

Assessing resources and risks

Once you've identified the strategies you'll use, you then assess the resources available to you to fulfill your business plan. This is the fifth step in the preparatory process.

In any organization, there are a number of resources that you'll be able to use when preparing a business plan. Five common types of resources are your people, your assets, IT, distribution, and finance.

See each resource to find out more information.

People

Consider how many people you'll need to make your plan a reality. Also think about what skills they should have and what training they'll need. Decide if you'll need to recruit people to your department in order to fulfill the plan.

For example, Mike, a creative manager at an advertising firm, has a plan to create a new online collaborative tool. To do this he needs people with a lot of programming experience.

Assets

Take note of the machinery you have access to, as well as the work space. If these aren't adequate to fulfill your plan, you may need to seek additional resources of this type. Alternatively, it might be necessary to scale back your plan.

For example, Ted, an insurance company's manager, has a plan that will require a lot of floor space, a projector, and other AV equipment to be readily available. He checks which of these assets are on hand and which need to be acquired.

IT

Consider the information technology you have available to you. If these resources aren't adequate, identify the most cost-effective way of acquiring the IT resources needed to fulfill your plan.

Lise, a frozen food company's HR manager, needs 40 laptops with high speed Internet connections in order to fulfill her plan. She meets with the company's IT manager to make sure these will be available.

Distribution

Consider the advantages and disadvantages of the distribution channels available to you. Depending on the product or service you're proposing, your distribution might work best entirely online. Or you may need to use agents or other intermediaries to get your products to market.

For example, V., the Sales Department head at an agricultural equipment retailer, discovers that direct shipping with an external logistics company best suits the needs of his new business plan.

Finance

Finance is crucial to the effective implementation of any business plan. Consider what financing you'll require to implement your plan. Make budgets for the coming years and, if necessary, seek out external sources of financing.

Grant, a chemical firm's production manager, finds that elements of his plan will cost hundreds of thousands of dollars, and that the firm will need to secure loans to cover these costs.

Having assessed resources, the sixth and final step in the preparatory process for developing your business plan is to identify the risks involved. Every plan will have some risks. It's crucial that you acknowledge any risks your business plan entails, so you should create a contingency plan to deal with these risks becoming reality. Identify the three most likely market risks associated with your type of plan and list them as part of the plan.

Riley, the assembly line manager at a canned foods company, prepares to develop a business plan. Having done everything else in the preparatory process, she identifies the risks involved in pursuing her plan. Her plan involves overhauling the plant's equipment and retraining employees so that productivity gains can be made.

Riley is quick to acknowledge that her plan contains some risks. It's possible that the new equipment will have initial troubles which could negatively impact productivity. She plans to bring the new equipment online

Business Planning

incrementally so that if it isn't working properly, production isn't halted.

As part of the business plan, she lists the three most likely risks involved in its implementation: the new equipment having problems; staff opposition to retraining; and the actual training being less effective than anticipated.

Once you've completed each of the six steps in preparing to develop your business plan, you can then start working on the structure of the plan. By following these preparatory steps, you're more likely to create an effective business plan.

Question

Which examples illustrate the assessing resources and risks step of preparing to develop a business plan?

Options:

1. Elliot includes a contingency plan in case there are problems with his business plan for the Sales Department of an insurance company

2. Liz consults other department heads about her goals for the Sales Department at an electronics company

3. Bernadette does an IT audit of the Advertising Department at a supermarket chain in preparation for her plan's implementation

4. Stan includes a strategy in his business plan that will suit how staff in his department in an IT firm work

Answer

Option 1: This option is correct. When identifying risks involved in your business plan, you should always include a contingency plan. If things go wrong, you then have a second plan to fall back on.

Option 2: This option is incorrect. This is an action taken as part of the establishing goals step in preparing to develop a plan.

Option 3: This option is correct. IT is one of the resources you should assess in preparation for developing your business plan.

Option 4: This option is incorrect. This is an action taken when identifying strategies for your business plan, the previous step in preparing to develop a business plan.

Learning aid - **Preparing to Develop Your Business Plan**

Take each step, in order, to help you prepare to develop your business plan.

Business plan step	Explanation
1. Define your mission	Organize your thoughts by considering the elements of a business plan, the opportunity, the solution, the execution, and the outcomes.
2. Do research	Identify critical issues related to your plan and ensure your ideas align with organizational strategy. Undertake a situation analysis, an external analysis, and a gap analysis and consider what your customer wants.
3. Establish goals	Be realistic about what you can achieve in implementing your business plan. Consider whether your goals conflict with those of other departments' plans.
4. Identify strategies to meet goals	Make sure the strategies you adopt to pursue your plan's goals clearly link to your department or organization's environment.
5. Assess resources	Assess the resources available to you, including people, assets, IT, distribution, and finance.
6. Identify risks	Acknowledge any risks your business plan entails and create a contingency plan to deal with these risks becoming reality. Identify the three most likely market risks associated with your type of plan and list them as part of the plan.

Guidelines for creating an effective business plan
The parts of a business plan

Business plans vary significantly depending on their primary purpose. When you've collected all the information you need to create a plan, you should then tailor the plan to its intended audience. For example, if you're with a startup seeking investment, your plan should target investors. Similarly, if your plan is for an established department in a large organization, you should make sure it will appeal to senior management.

A business plan typically comprises four major parts. These are the executive summary, the market opportunity, the implementation, and the contingencies. Each of these four major parts of your plan should be completed with your audience in mind.

See each business plan part to find out more information.

Executive summary

The executive summary is an abstract of your business plan. It lists everything you'll detail in subsequent sections of the plan. It describes your proposed idea – whether it's a new product or service, a new process, or some kind of expansion. It then summarizes the purpose, management, operations, marketing, and finances for this idea.

Market opportunity

The market opportunity describes the unmet need or want your product, service, process, or expansion will fulfill. It also presents evidence that there is consumer demand for whatever you are proposing. This section typically includes credible market research about your target market. This section should also describe ways of testing the potential popularity of any product or service you want to introduce.

Implementation

Implementation is the how-to section of your business plan. It details steps you'll take in the areas of marketing, operations and finances, and people. Your marketing subsection builds on market research presented. Your financial plan will include costs to launch, operate, market, and finance the idea, along with realistic estimates of revenue for the coming few years. The people section describes key personnel and why they're suitable for their roles.

Contingencies

In the contingencies section, you'll outline those things that are most likely to go wrong as you implement your plan. It also includes details of how you'll respond to any problems that arise. While you can't plan for every contingency, this section illustrates your willingness and ability to deal with unforeseen adverse circumstances.

When creating your own business plan, consider each of the major parts in turn and be clear about what each comprises. You must then present each of the major parts in a way that's appealing to your audience.

Question

Match each description to the business plan part it describes.

Options:

A. This is the how-to section of a business plan that details steps taken in the areas of marketing, operations and finances, and people

B. This is an abstract of the business plan that reviews its purpose, management, operations, and finances

C. This section outlines what may go wrong with a plan and how problems will be dealt with

D. This section describes the unmet need a product or service will fulfill and presents evidence that there's consumer demand for it

Targets:
1. Executive summary
2. Market opportunity
3. Implementation
4. Contingencies

Answer

The executive summary is an abstract of the business plan that reviews its purpose, management, operations, and finances.

The market opportunity details the need a product or service fulfills and contains research showing probable demand.

Implementation is the part of the plan which details the steps taken in the areas of marketing, operations and finance, and people.

Contingencies is the section that details what could go wrong with the plan and what will be done if something does go wrong.

Business plan review

When a business plan is being presented to an audience, many issues may arise and affect how the audience responds. For example, Matthew, Heidi, and Omar are senior executives at a camping equipment company. They're reviewing a business plan from the company's product development unit, which describes the unit's intended foray into generators for the camping market.

Heidi, Matthew, and Omar have the final say as to whether the plan goes ahead. Follow along as they comment on the business plan.

Heidi: Way too long! All this information...it's just not coherent.

Heidi is concerned.

Matthew: Agreed. The summary doesn't even tell us what we need to know. I'm still asking – what exactly do these guys want to do?

Matthew is slightly annoyed.

Omar: The implementation section? Zero information about marketing needs. And growth projections are just not realistic.

Omar is concerned.

Heidi: Well, I certainly can't support the plan as it stands. Frankly, it makes me wonder – does anyone in product development know what they're doing?

Heidi is angry.

Matthew: Me neither. I just don't know what it's proposing.

Omar: Makes three of us! It's not supportable. Not the way it is, anyway. Needs a lot more work before I'd be comfortable signing off on it.

Omar is serious.

Question

Which elements of the plan that Heidi, Matthew, and Omar reviewed do you think could be improved upon?

Options:

1. The business plan could include more details in every section
2. The business plan could be shorter

3. The plan should be more optimistic about projected growth

4. The summary could be clearer and better written

Answer

Option 1: This option is incorrect. Business plans should be kept short so that the real point of them isn't lost among irrelevant data.

Option 2: This option is correct. An effective business plan is typically short. Putting in too much information can undermine the plan's effectiveness with its audience.

Option 3: This option is incorrect. When providing projections of growth or other outcomes, it's important to be realistic and not exaggerate the plan's effects.

Option 4: This option is correct. In order to gain approval, a business plan's summary should be clear and well-written.

Heidi, Matthew, and Omar have been presented with a business plan they can't support. Because of weaknesses in the plan, the product development unit will lose out on the support it needs for new ideas. First off, the plan is too long, with seemingly too many irrelevant details. The executive summary, the first part everyone reads, isn't well written. It doesn't include the specifics of its goals, and it includes unrealistic projections.

Effective business plans capture their audience's attention. This increases the likelihood a plan will be accepted.

They capture their audience by presenting a compelling narrative. Instead of lists of facts or figures, they tell a story the audience wants to hear.

Such documents don't need to be very long. What's most important is that they're focused and clear, with the most relevant issues addressed succinctly.

Business plan guidelines

By following certain guidelines, you can create an effective business plan that should capture your target audience's attention and, ultimately, likely get their approval. The first of the guidelines is keep it short. Make sure to pay special attention to the executive summary. Also, tell a compelling story and ensure your plan fits the business need. Next, be realistic and specific. And, finally with regard to page layout and writing style, make it reader-friendly.

The first guideline for creating an effective business plan is to keep it short. Often people fill their business plans with superfluous facts and figures. They include absolutely every detail related to the business, the market, and competitors, instead of focusing on the most relevant. Including these extra details can drown out the specific points you're trying to convey to your audience. Don't include too much information.

Reflect

Why do you think you should pay special attention to the executive summary when creating a business plan?

Write down your response or enter it in a text file in your word-processor application (or in a text editor such as Notepad) and save it to your hard drive for later viewing.

There are many reasons you may have given for why you should pay attention to the executive summary. The summary represents your opening argument. It's the most important section of the plan, as it's the first section your audience reads. You should write your executive summary first and spend time improving it. Be short and persuasive. Clearly define your business idea and the logic behind it. This will provide a theme for the rest of the plan.

Ideally, your executive summary shouldn't be longer than a page or two. If the summary becomes longer than this, it's likely to lose focus.

Consider this example. A long established catering company has created a business plan in order to attract new investment to help it expand both its range and its reach in international markets. However, its executive summary is over ten pages long.

The plan's audience, a group of investors, typically sees numerous business plans every week. When the group comes across an executive summary that's overly long, it's more likely to dismiss the plan without investing. The catering company loses out on the investment it needs because it didn't create a succinct executive summary.

The next guideline for creating an effective business plan is to tell a compelling story. Compiling an assortment of facts and figures is not enough to ensure your audience buys into your plan. You must construct a narrative that draws in your audience. This narrative should flow smoothly but also indicate to your audience you've considered other avenues and contingencies.

For example, an appliance manufacturer's R&D Department puts together a business plan for a new product. However, instead of just focusing exclusively on market share or growth, the business plan tells the story of the product's likely impact on consumers.

The R&D Department's business plan clearly illustrates why consumers will flock to the product by showing the specific applications and implications of the product for customers. This single product is pitched to replace several common kitchen appliances.

A vivid description of the product's likely effects helps capture the imagination of senior management and ultimately secures management's support for the plan.

Question

How can you improve the chances of your business plan being approved by senior management?

Options:

1. Weed out irrelevant information and keep the plan to three pages

2. Make sure that the summary provides a clear outline of issues covered in the plan

3. Include all information that you think is related to your idea

4. Put your plan in context by telling how it will change things

5. Exaggerate to draw your audience into your plan's central idea

Answer

Option 1: This option is correct. An easy mistake to make when creating a business plan is including too much information.

Option 2: This option is correct. The executive summary is the first part of your plan that your audience will read, so write it first and spend time making sure it's well written.

Option 3: This option is incorrect. You should keep your business plan short, only including information absolutely relevant to pitching your idea.

Option 4: This option is correct. A set of facts and figures isn't enough to sell your plan, so construct a compelling narrative to hang your plan on.

Option 5: This option is incorrect. It's important to be realistic when creating your business plan. Exaggerating in a plan is not going to win over management.

The fourth guideline is that your business plan should fit the business need. Be clear about the business need your plan is addressing. If the plan is for internal approval, it will vary from plans aimed at seeking investment or securing a loan externally. Typically, a more polished presentation will be expected if your plan is for an external audience. No single business plan type fits all business needs.

For example, a construction company's managers have created a business plan. They aim to secure a loan from a financial institution. They hope that this source of capital can be used to expand the company's operations.

The plan is given as part of a loan application to a financial institution. The plan fails to provide enough assurances that the substantial loan is likely to be paid off. For this reason, the loan application is denied.

The construction company should have addressed the needs of the lenders when creating the business plan.

Question

What do you think the construction company's managers need to do to create an effective plan?

Options:

1. Focus on how the plan will help the company expand into new markets

2. Provide clear assurances that the loan will be serviced and paid off in full

3. Create an impression that the plan's risks are minimal

Answer

Option 1: This option is incorrect. A financial institution is primarily concerned with whether a loan will be paid off, not how well the company will fare otherwise.

Option 2: This is the correct option. This is the essential information that should be included in a plan when a lender is the audience.

Option 3: This option is incorrect. When targeting a lender with a business plan, you should be honest about risks involved.

The next guideline is that your business plan must be realistic and specific. It should include achievable goals for its time line and an accurate budget. You'll want to impress your audience, but if your goals aren't achievable, your business plan will lose credibility. Its goals should also be measurable. Include tasks, deadlines, forecasts, budgets, and other metrics that can be checked as the plan progresses. Without these metrics, it may be difficult to ascertain later if the plan has been fulfilled.

For example, say a consumer electronics firm's sales team puts together a business plan for senior management. Some of their projected sales are based on the firm making several advances that are unlikely without an unfeasibly large injection of capital.

The plan also doesn't contain enough measurable outcomes. Apart from sales projections, the sales team has neglected to include metrics that will indicate whether the plan is succeeding. These oversights are liable to jeopardize the plan's acceptance.

Senior management sends the plan back and tells the team to put together a more realistic set of figures and lay out more metrics for the plan's progress.

The final guideline for creating an effective business plan is to make it reader-friendly. Work on the page layout and writing style. Allow for adequate spacing and use a font that's easy to read. Also use a simple and clear structure for headings and subheadings so the document is easy to navigate. Write the document clearly and concisely. Avoid long sentences and convoluted explanations. Consider whether to use a traditional document format or a more dynamic computer-based format.

The managers of a newly-formed travel company have created a business plan in the hope of gaining investment. They initially created a printed document including the plan. Although this is well laid out and clearly written, they find it quickly becomes obsolete as new ideas are included in their plans for the business.

To make it easier to update their business plan, they compile it in the form of a computer-based presentation. This format allows them to quickly alter sections of the plan where necessary. The digital format also suits a lot of the investors who are used to reviewing documents on their smartphones and tablet PCs.

Question

Which guidelines should you follow when creating an effective business plan?

Options:

1. Delegate responsibility for different parts of the plan to others
2. Make sure the business plan is laid out in a way that the managers will find easy to read
3. Be realistic and specific about the goals of your business plan
4. Include all the information you've collected in the business plan
5. Make sure the plan is tailored to the business's need for investment

Answer

Option 1: This option is incorrect. Although there may be no problem with delegation, it's not a guideline for creating an effective business plan.

Option 2: This option is correct. Concentrate on the page layout and writing style so your plan is readable. Alternatively, present it in a dynamic digital format.

Option 3: This option is correct. Your plan must include goals and projects that are realistic. It should also include metrics for progress.

Option 4: This option is incorrect. Your plan should be short and exclude any information that isn't directly related to your core business ideas and goals.

Option 5: This option is correct. If you're creating the plan for internal use, it will differ to plans created when seeking investment or securing loans externally.

x

Learning aid - Business Plan Guidelines

By following these guidelines, you can create an effective business plan to which people respond favorably.

Business Planning

Business plan guideline	Explanation
Keep it short	Don't include every detail related to the business, market, and competitors
	Only include important details, which provide focus and clarity
Pay attention to the executive summary	Write the summary first and spend time perfecting it
	Be short and persuasive
	Clearly define your business idea and the logic behind it
Tell a compelling story	Compiling facts and figures isn't enough to ensure buy-in to your plan
	Construct a narrative that draws in your audience
Make sure the plan fits the business need	Form should follow function
	Internally-aimed business plans contain different information to those aimed at seeking investment or loans
Be realistic and specific	Include achievable goals for your plan's time line and budget
	Goals should be measurable
	Include tasks, deadlines, forecasts, budgets, and other metrics
Make it reader-friendly	Work on the page layout and writing style
	Allow for adequate spacing and use a font that makes it easy to read
	Use a simple and clear structure for headings and subheadings
	Write the document clearly and concisely
	Avoid long sentences and convoluted explanations

Learning aid - Creating a Business Plan

When creating your business plan, consider what you will include for each of these parts in turn, as well as how you can tailor the details for the business plan's audience.

Business plan parts

Sorin Dumitrascu

Business plan part	Explanation
Executive summary	The executive summary is an abstract of your business plan. It lists everything you'll detail in subsequent sections of the plan. It describes your organization, business venture, product, or service. It then summarizes its purpose, management, operations, marketing, and finances.
Market opportunity	The market opportunity describes the unmet need your product, service, process, or expansion will fulfill. It also presents evidence of consumer demand for your product or service. This section usually includes credible market research about your target market. It also describes ways of testing the potential popularity of your product or service.
Implementation	Implementation is the how-to section of your business plan. It details steps you'll take in the areas of marketing, operations and finances, and people to fulfill your plan. Your marketing subsection builds on market research presented. Your financial plan will include costs to launch, operate, market, and finance the business, along with estimates of revenue for the coming few years. The people section describes key personnel and why they're suitable for their roles.
Contingencies	The contingencies section outlines those things that are most likely to go wrong as you implement your business plan, and includes details of how you'll respond to any problems. While you can't plan for every single contingency, this section illustrates your willingness and ability to deal with unforeseen adverse circumstances.

CHAPTER TWO
Performing Key Analyses

The results of an internal analysis
Using internal analysis for business plans

People develop business plans for many reasons – it could be to seek funding for a project, evaluate future growth potential, or perhaps establish a new business partnership. So a business plan is essentially a formal framework for gaining the support you need for your business idea or project. Your plan should lay out how you'll achieve your objectives within a specified time frame – often less than three years.

A business plan will typically include an executive summary, information on market opportunities, the implementation details of the plan, and any necessary contingencies to account for known or unforeseen developments.

See each item to learn more about it.

Executive summary

The executive summary is a broad overview of your business idea. It should outline high-level details about your organization and highlights of your business idea or project and its goals.

The executive summary is often considered the most important section of the plan and usually comes first – although it's best written last.

Market opportunities

The market opportunities for your business idea must outline the current – or future – gap it will fill in the market. You can present evidence from your market research to support the product or service, and verify that customers will be willing to pay for it.

You should also include information on your competitors, and pricing for your product or service.

Implementation

Your implementation plan will outline the action steps to achieve your goals. It should cover marketing, operational activities, financial costs, and the people required to bring the product or service to market.

The marketing implementation plan builds on market research. You should include your competitive niche – that is, how you'll be better than your competitors.

In terms of the people involved, you can describe who'll be responsible for developing, marketing, and operating the project, and why their backgrounds and skills make them the right people to make the plan succeed.

Contingencies

It's unlikely that absolutely everything will go according to plan. So the contingencies section of your business plan should outline an assessment of the likely risks and barriers to success. You should show that you've explored different scenarios about what could go wrong with the plan.

Question

As you develop your business plan, it's important to perform a situational analysis. This is an analysis of your internal and external environments to identify factors that may impact your company's performance.

What do you think are benefits of conducting a situational analysis?

Options:

1. It helps you consider how your business idea will unfold in the future

2. It clarifies the economic conditions within which the organization operates

3. It enables you to better understand potential issues and their impact on your plan

4. It defines the market share you will achieve

5. It helps you understand your investors better

Answer

A situational analysis can't tell you what market share you'll achieve or understand your investors. Benefits of a situational analysis include helping you consider how your business idea will unfold in the future, allowing you to plan effectively. An analysis also helps clarify the internal and external environmental conditions, and helps you understand how your plan may work under different contexts.

A situational analysis helps you identify factors that will impact your company's performance.

You consider how your idea might work in different contexts. For instance, if you're developing a plan for a new initiative, think about possible internal issues – like lack of resources – and threats to reaching your objectives, like possible competitors.

Staying current with the external and internal environments can not only help you develop new business ideas, but can help you refine an idea you've already come up with.

Performing situational analyses has benefits for business planning:
- it helps you determine how your business idea will unfold in the future, and thereby helps inform what you should put into your plan
- it enables you to identify your organization's resources and capabilities so that you can leverage these in your plan, and
- it helps you explore any important issues that might impact the plan, so you can include any threats or opportunities

Conducting an internal analysis

A robust situational analysis will include an internal analysis to identify the strengths and weaknesses of your company. It'll also include an external analysis to identify the external opportunities and threats to your company. In practice, both analyses should be parallel activities when preparing your business plan. This topic will focus on the internal analysis.

The purpose of an internal analysis is to identify the potential of your company. A robust internal analysis should point out the significance and impact of external factors on your business. You'll then be in a better position to respond to them. Assessing strengths and weaknesses should then highlight your company's potential to grow, compete effectively in the marketplace, and be commercially viable.

An internal analysis can help you evaluate an existing business plan. Alternatively, you can carry out an internal analysis to develop a new business idea. Regardless, an internal analysis will help determine whether or not your plan or idea might work in actual practice.

There are many issues to consider during your internal analysis. An example would be a review of the products and services your company provides. You should also consider your customer profile, your competitive base, and the values your company holds regarding growth and expansion. It's also important to consider what your benchmark for successful performance is.

Determine your company's strengths and weaknesses. Then consider how they apply to your vision statement for next year. How will the strengths get you closer to your goals? How will the weaknesses hold you back?

For instance, suppose your vision is to double sales for next year and make your product better known outside the local area. You identify your strengths as a quality product and customer loyalty. However, you identify your weaknesses as poor marketing and advertising. You can then explore ways to improve on the weaknesses and capitalize on the strengths.

Question

What is an internal analysis?

Options:

1. It's an activity that identifies the impact of external factors on your business

2. It examines the capabilities of the company's operations

3. It considers the types of customers a company sells to

4. It investigates the opportunities and threats to your company

5. It's an activity that should be carried out before the external analysis

Answer

Option 1: This option is correct. An internal analysis examines how your company currently responds to external factors.

Option 2: This option is correct. An internal analysis can determine if your company's operations are a strength or a weakness.

Option 3: This option is correct. An internal analysis will examine your customer profile.

Option 4: This option is incorrect. Opportunities and threats are examined as part of the external analysis.

Option 5: This option is incorrect. An internal analysis can be done in parallel with an external analysis.

Market strategy

There are four steps you can take when conducting an internal analysis – although the steps don't need to be carried out in any particular order. You should assess the company's market strategy and its resources. You also evaluate the organizational and management strategy, as well as your organization's financial position. Taking these steps can provide useful insights for a business plan or idea.

Assessing the market strategy is an important step in your internal analysis. A good place to start is to use company data on customer sales, product revenue analysis, and the geographic distribution of your target customers. You can then extrapolate trends over time to support your evaluation.

See each analysis type for examples.

Customer sales

An example of a customer sales review would be determining where the sales are, their value, and which areas are growing faster or slower than others.

Product revenue

A product revenue analysis could involve identifying how your current products are rated by your customers. You may find that some of your products are outdated. You could also look at the last time you launched a new product and how it was received by customers.

Geographic distribution

A geographic distribution review will tell you where you sell the most of your product or service. It'll give you an age profile of your customers. You could also determine if some areas are over- saturated with marketing or require additional attention.

You can continue your evaluation by asking a number of questions about the data:

- What's the profile of your key customers and what products or services have they purchased?
- What has been the extent of their purchases?
- How have these purchases been affected by product or service prices and sales, advertising, and your distribution practices?
- What has been the net impact on revenue?

In answering these key questions, you'll gain valuable information about the strengths and weaknesses of the company's current market strategy. You can then use the results to examine your portfolio of products or services to determine the best strategies for you to follow going forward. This type of information will inform the development of your business idea or plan.

Question

How can you assess your company's market strategy?

Options:

1. Review company data on customer sales
2. Conduct a product revenue analysis
3. Analyze geographic distribution
4. Review the products of your competitors
5. Assess external market conditions

Answer

Option 1: This option is correct. A market strategy on customer sales will tell you the value of sales.

Option 2: This option is correct. A product review analysis will tell you how your current products are rated by your customers.

Option 3: This option is correct. A geographic distribution analysis will determine where you sell the most products.

Option 4: This option is incorrect. A market strategy is for your own product, not your competitors'. Option 5: This option is incorrect. A market strategy is part of your company's internal analysis, not its external analysis.

Consider Eric, a manager at a manufacturing company, Phlogistix. His manager has asked him to evaluate a business idea that was proposed in the last strategic planning session. The idea is to develop a new home cleaning appliance.

Eric needs to perform an internal analysis to determine whether Phlogistix can realistically implement this idea. He begins by examining Phlogistix's current market strategy. Eric finds that Phlogistix currently promotes cleaning appliances through a large network of distributors.

Eric takes a historical perspective to identify key trends and previous cause-and-effect relationships. He consults company records and becomes concerned that Phlogistix has had difficulty gaining market share in the home appliances market in the past. The company tried to launch a similar device once before but ran into interoperability issues with leading software that most businesses and consumers use.

Eric considers current sales figures to decide whether it's more sensible to upgrade existing appliances. Customer sales analysis indicates customers are a stable source of revenue. A product revenue analysis reveals that the current portfolio of appliances are yielding adequate revenue. A geographic sales analysis identifies the most profitable area to bring the appliance to market.

So how will Eric reflect his findings in his business plan? First, it's advisable to note all his findings in the plan. He can then check to see if the interoperability issues were ever worked out, and if so, how much effort it took his predecessor.

Eric discovers it was a problem that the company cannot afford to run into again. He decides to add more details to his business plan about how he'll avoid or manage this type of issue without expending an inordinate amount of resources.

Resources

Another step in an internal analysis is assessing your company's resources. You need to identify the resources most important to the business, such as research and development employees, or top-of-the-line equipment. This allows you to focus on the resources that are a source of competitive advantage to

the company. By identifying the unique selling points of your organization, you'll be able to incorporate them into your developing business plan or idea.

A unique selling point is something your company can give customers over and above competitors. For instance, a bank may set itself apart from its competitors by offering longer hours of operation for customers.

You should compare your company's distinguishing competencies and specific strengths with your competitors'. For instance, do you have better staffing capabilities to be open longer hours? Similarly, you can identify your weaknesses that provide a source of competitive disadvantage to your competitors.

Assessing resources can highlight your company's readiness to implement a new product or service. Remember Eric? He's now reviewing his company's resources. He identifies the company's strengths as having many qualified developers in the R&D Department to create a quality cleaning appliance. He realizes this is Phlogistix's unique selling point. Another strength is a strong international marketing team to promote the new appliance.

However, he identifies a weakness in the company's resources. Phlogistix outsources its electronics to another company, and the relationship with this company has been strained in recent years due to a large number of faulty chips. This undermines the ability of the developers to create a quality product.

Eric decides to add details to his business plan about how he'll seek out a stronger and more reputable electronics partner.

Question

What is the purpose of assessing your company's resources?

Options:

1. To determine the resources and capabilities that are a source of competitive advantage to the company

2. To identify competitors' unique selling points so your company can generate ideas for more competitive products

3. To determine which markets your resources are concentrated in

Answer

Option 1: This is the correct option. When doing an internal analysis, it's important to examine the resources and capabilities of your company to identify its strengths and weaknesses. Then you can draw on the best resources and capabilities to develop your business idea.

Option 2: This option is incorrect. Assessing your company's resources helps you determine what you have at your disposal for making your business plan or idea successful. It helps you determine the unique selling points of your organization, which can guide you in writing a plan that takes advantage of these.

Option 3: This option is incorrect. It's more important to find out the strengths and weaknesses in your organization's resources and capabilities so that you can build a plan that takes those into account.

Organization and management strategy

Another key step is to evaluate the organizational and management strategies. During this phase of your analysis, you need to review the organizational structure of your company and its subunits. You can achieve this by observing, reviewing key policies and procedures, and holding interviews with senior managers.

For example, consider the innovation culture in the organization. Are employees given freedom to be creative and propose ideas – for instance, through a contest to develop new ideas, with a prize for the best one? Or are employees expected to fall in line with how things have always been done in the company?

It's also worth considering the quality of managers in the organization. For instance, determine if your company has strong leaders, and if employees are motivated by good performance rewards and incentives. Strong leaders are supportive and typically have an open door policy.

Also, be aware of your organization's processes and procedures. For instance, is information readily available to employees, and are the product development procedures updated regularly?

Eric is now evaluating Phlogistix's organizational and management strategies. His research has highlighted some important factors:

- the company's structure allows employees to regularly contribute ideas to improve products
- the company's culture encourages and supports new initiatives
- managers are hands-on and he feels that his initiative would gather management support rather than face obstacles, and

Business Planning

- the company provides competitive incentives and rewards for employees to get involved in projects

After considering his company's organizational and management strategies, Eric considers how they'll affect his plan. He's impressed with management's enthusiasm for product development. There have been a large number of new products approved in the last year. Eric is now confident that, with a good business plan, he'll gain the support he needs for his new product.

Question

Which of these areas would form part of the organizational and management strategy evaluation?

Options:

1. Assessing innovation culture
2. Determining management support
3. Reviewing rewards and incentives
4. Completing a product analysis
5. Identifying unique selling points

Answer

Option 1: This option is correct. Assessing the innovation culture will help you determine the extent of innovation in your workplace.

Option 2: This option is correct. The level of management support for innovation and development can determine the likely support for your business plan.

Option 3: This option is correct. The level of rewards and incentives will influence employees' motivation to innovate.

Option 4: This option is incorrect. A product analysis is part of assessing the market strategy.

Option 5: This option is incorrect. Identifying unique selling points is part of assessing resources.

Financial position

Evaluating your organization's financial position is a fundamental step in undertaking any new initiative.

As part of a financial analysis, you'll examine the company's assets and liabilities to determine whether the company is currently profitable. A review of your company's revenue sources and expenses will tell you if money is available for your business idea. For instance, do profits come from products or services?

You can also examine if the company has the required assets to develop a new product or service – or whatever your idea may be. For instance, an asset could be a dedicated testing facility used for new product development.

You can also determine if you're missing something fundamental to your business plan, such as government licenses.

You can also consider if the organization can actually support this type of initiative given its financial position. Maybe the company has had a bad year, or is planning a merger that will consume any available cash. If funds are available, your business plan can then reconcile money to support your plan's objectives.

Eric is now evaluating the financial position at Phlogistix. To determine if it's profitable, he notes the revenues. Most notably, Phlogistix received $10 million from its portfolio of products and a $2 million investment for R&D.

However, Eric is concerned that Phlogistix doesn't have all the financial resources to replace the third- party provider that it outsources parts to, which he determined was a weakness during his resource review. He updates the plan accordingly, and addresses his concerns with the management team.

Case Study: Question 1 of 2
Scenario

You're a product manager with an advertising company. You have an idea to develop and market a new translation service to international clients. In order to put the idea into action, you first need to perform an internal analysis to determine whether your company can see the proposal through.

Answer the questions in order.

Question

What types of information will your internal analysis yield?

Options:

1. Weaknesses in your company's international market strategy
2. Your international competitive advantage in advertising
3. The organization's current ability to adapt to changing external conditions in the advertising industry
4. Your company's current revenue and expenses from activities abroad 5. Historical trends in the advertising industry for translation services
6. Key strengths of your competitors

Answer

Option 1: This option is correct. A good internal analysis will identify both strengths and weaknesses in the company's current market strategy.

Option 2: This option is correct. An internal analysis of company resources should tell you what your key differentiators and unique selling points are.

Option 3: This option is correct. A thorough internal analysis should determine the current management strategy for dealing with changing external conditions.

Option 4: This option is correct. An internal analysis isn't complete without reviewing the company's current financial information, including revenue and expenses.

Option 5: This option is incorrect. An internal analysis helps to examine your own company. An external analysis will examine industry trends.

Option 6: This option is incorrect. An internal analysis helps you examine your own company. An external analysis will examine your competitors.

Case Study: Question 2 of 2

Scenario

You're a product manager with an advertising company. You have an idea to develop and market a new translation service to international clients. In order to put the idea into action, you first need to perform an internal analysis to determine whether your company can see the proposal through.

Answer the questions in order.

Question

How can the results of your internal analysis inform your business plan?

Options:

1. You note the company's product development fund, which can help you write the financial section of the plan

2. Your analysis can determine if international customers are a growing or declining source of revenue 3. You'll know which resources your plan should focus on to give you a competitive advantage on a large scale

4. You'll consider current management challenges and amend your business plan accordingly 5. You'll have a better understanding of how customers will respond to your products within the next three years

6. You'll understand the competitive advantage of other products in the marketplace

Answer

Option 1: This option is correct. An analysis of the company's financial position, such as current assets and liabilities, will tell you what funds are available to you.

Option 2: This option is correct. Reviewing the target customer as part of the market strategy can help determine if the business plan is feasible.

Option 3: This option is correct. Studying various resources, such as people or equipment, as part of an assessment of company resources can tell you what your competitive advantage is. In turn, you can try to leverage those strengths in the plan.

Option 4: This option is correct. Identifying weaknesses in organizational and management strategy can help you find ways to improve the capabilities of management.

Option 5: This option is incorrect. An internal analysis can only assess past and current habits of customers. The needs and behavior of customers is always evolving.

Option 6: This option is incorrect. An internal analysis is an assessment of your own company's resources, not an assessment of your competitors'.

Learning aid - Conducting an Internal Analysis

Use the table to help identify the strengths and weakness in your company. You can print this document, or recreate the table in a word processing or spreadsheet application and use it to complete this activity. There are four key steps to conducting an internal analysis.

Steps	Descriptions
Assess market strategy	Examine company data on customer sales, product revenue analysis, and geographical distribution
	Extrapolate trends over time to support your evaluation
	Determine profile of key customers
	Determine the impact on revenue
	Use the results to examine your portfolio of products or services to determine the best strategies to follow
Assess resources	Identify the resources most important to the business – such as research and development employees or top-of-the-line equipment
	Focus on the resources that are a source of competitive advantage to the company
	Assessing resources can highlight a company's readiness to implement a new product or service
Evaluate organization and management strategy	Look at the organizational structure of your company and its subunits
	Observe, review key policies and procedures, and hold interviews with senior managers
	Assess learning culture and management practices
	Determines the potential support or blockers for your business plan
Evaluate your organization's financial position	Examine the company's current revenue, expenses, assets, and liabilities to determine whether the company is currently profitable
	Determine if money is available for your business idea

Conduct an external analysis

Organizations don't operate in isolation. Their success or failure can be affected by external factors such as economic downturns. An external situational analysis examines the important factors that can change the course of your business. Such factors include government policies, consumer sentiment, and new technology. These are potential threats or opportunities that your business has little or no control of. It's therefore important to be prepared by including this information in your business plan.

A thorough analysis of the external environment can improve your business plan and help you predict the conditions in which your business may have to operate in the future. Such environmental factors may be macro or micro in nature.

See each environmental factor to learn more.

Macro

Macro factors are decided by government economic policy and affect the broader economy. Examples include the level of inflation, interest rates, and exchange rates. The main factors fall into four groups: political, economic, societal, and technological.

Micro

Micro factors include stakeholders, such as customers, employees, shareholders, and competitors.

Regional and industrial policy are also considered micro factors because they directly affect businesses. For instance, the availability of grants or infrastructure may influence where a business is located.

A PEST analysis is often used to examine the key macro factors – that is, the political, economic, societal, and technological factors. These factors are inextricably linked. Together they reveal many of the external environmental factors influencing your company's performance and, subsequently, how you develop your business plan.

See each type of factor to learn more.

Political

Company operations are affected by political factors such as corporate tax, monetary policy, foreign trade policy, competition law, regulation, and government bureaucracy. Education policy also impacts a business's ability to recruit qualified employees. Such influences can complicate or delay business development.

Economic

Company profitability is influenced by bull or bear markets, infrastructure, inflation, interest rates, fuel prices, and exchange rates. These factors affect the price of raw materials and labor, and the ability to sell goods and services. Some businesses are more prone to business cycles than others – for instance, the leisure industry is more susceptible than the food service sector.

Societal

Plans can be affected by societal factors such as the average amount of time people work every week, which typically influences the amount of free time they have to spend elsewhere.

Consumer spending is also often directly related to demographics and social norms – for instance, how many people are currently employed as opposed to unemployed? What do people spend their time doing? Do they spend most of their free time with family and religious or community groups? Have most people gone to university and, if so, what is the average income?

Technological

Company profitability is influenced by technological advances, as technology can have a sudden impact on an economy. The availability of government funding, investment by competitors into R&D, and new production methods can impact your external environment. These factors can indicate whether any technological changes should be anticipated.

Consumer spending and the time it takes for people to buy into technology can impact consumer demand. A business plan must therefore examine how long it will take for a new product to filter into the market.

Question

What factors would you consider when doing an external analysis for business planning?

Options:

1. Government cash injections into the economy
2. The economic state of the country
3. A profile of working mothers and their level of disposable income
4. Advances in technology that may support your proposed business plan
5. Whether the company's marketing team has the capability to market your business idea
6. The company's current assets and liabilities

Answer

Option 1: This option is correct. Government monetary policy is a political factor that should be included in your PEST analysis.

Option 2: This option is correct. Your PEST analysis should consider economic factors, as these can impact the readiness of consumers to spend money.

Option 3: This option is correct. Demographics and the level of spending and saving influence disposable income. This should be included in your PEST analysis as it may affect the profitability of your business idea.

Option 4: This option is correct. The technological analysis may uncover new technologies that may support your proposed plans.

Option 5: This option is incorrect. An assessment of company resources is carried out as part of an internal analysis. An external analysis looks at political, economic, societal, and technological factors.

Option 6: This option is incorrect. Financial assessment is part of an internal analysis. An external analysis looks at political, economic, societal, and technological factors.

External analysis: scenario planning

As part of an external analysis, you may use scenario planning. Scenario planning can help you visualize the future environment for your business. It adds additional value to your PEST analysis by outlining different scenarios of how your business might operate under different political, economic, societal, and technological conditions. It's a structured approach to dealing with unpredictable events you may encounter.

Good scenario planning will help tell the full story behind the business plan and provide the structure for more realistic forecasts.

When presenting your business plan, you'll be able to convey a greater understanding of the external environment and how it impacts your company's activities.

There are four steps to scenario planning. First, pinpoint the factors of high uncertainty and high impact. You can use a matrix to record the business impacts and uncertainty levels of various factors. Second, outline alternative scenarios for those factors. Third, select the three most likely scenarios, and finally, write the scenario descriptions.

See each step, in order, to learn more.

Pinpoint uncertainty and impact

You need to plan for the uncertainty of external factors and the impact on your business plan. Factors that seem certain and positive may later become irregular – for instance, the housing market may boom for 10 years, then become unstable.

Scenarios are developed around the factors that have the greatest uncertainty and the most impact on your business plan.

Outline alternative scenarios

You should include any environmental factors that have the greatest uncertainty and greatest risk to the business. You examine these factors and develop two or three detailed alternative scenarios for each. For instance, if you think the minimum wage could double in the next few months but you're not 100% sure, you should come up with an alternative scenario to deal with it.

Select three scenarios

Combining different possible scenario paths for each factor suggests many potential outcomes. Your goal should be to identify three or four important scenarios. You should choose scenarios that are realistic, diverse, and directly linked to any problems relating to your business plan.

Write scenario descriptions

Your scenario descriptions should be powerful descriptions that highlight the assumptions you've made, the relevant business context, and a time line for how the scenario could unfold.

Consider Eric, a manager at a manufacturing company, Phlogistix. His manager has asked him to evaluate a business idea to develop a new home cleaning appliance. Eric completes a PEST analysis matrix to determine the factors that will impact his company.

Eric identifies exchange rates and interest rates as high uncertainty, low impact. The availability of credit and rate of economic growth are low uncertainty, low impact. He also factors in disposable incomes and the rate of adoption of new technology as high uncertainty, high impact. Finally, the cost of parts for the appliance and the potential for mergers and acquisitions of competitors are low uncertainty, high impact.

For his scenario planning, Eric considers the most uncertain and riskiest factors to his business – disposable incomes and the rate of adoption of new technology.

Eric then writes his alternative scenarios for how the business must adapt under different circumstances. For example, how profitable can the cleaning appliance be if disposable incomes are low and the rate of adoption of the new technology is sluggish?

Eric finally selects three scenarios that he feels are most likely to impact his business planning and writes his scenario descriptions.

Question

What are appropriate ways to carry out scenario planning when doing an external analysis for business planning?

Options:

1. Develop scenarios around uncertain factors that could impact the business plan

2. Focus on factors with the highest uncertainty and greatest potential impact

3. Write scenario descriptions for three realistic scenarios

4. Consider factors with the highest certainty and most impact

5. Choose one scenario and focus on how it affects planning

Answer

Option 1: This option is correct. The objective of scenario planning is to determine how certain external factors might impact your business plan.

Option 2: This option is correct. The greatest risks to your business plan are highly uncertain factors that may impact your plan's success, such as fluctuating labor and materials costs.

Option 3: This option is correct. Describing three probable scenarios will help you visualize the possible outcomes under different external pressures and what you may need to do to mitigate any negative impact on your plan.

Option 4: This option is incorrect. You need to focus on the factors with the highest uncertainty and greatest impact.

Option 5: This option is incorrect. It's better to select a couple of scenarios to develop and use to describe how your plan may work out.

Market analysis: customer groups

After scenario planning for the broader political, economic, societal, and technological considerations, you can consider the market relevant to your business. Your marketing strategy – a key part of your business plan – identifies opportunities and threats that affect your strategy. The areas to cover in your market analysis are customer groups, competitors, and your industry.

The first part of your market analysis is customer groups. Marketing should focus on your customers rather than your products or services, making customers central to your business plan. Successful companies organize business activities that plan, price, promote, and distribute products and services that satisfy the wants and needs of customers.

To develop business plans that will be successful, you need to know what customers want, and how to best meet those needs. Engaging in customer and market research can help you achieve this:

- examine seasonal, geographic, and historic buying trends and identify opportunities to create substitutes for competitor products
- survey sales and marketing professionals to help determine trends in selling, sales strategies and tactics, and promotional opportunities
- analyze current distribution channels in order to find opportunities to enhance the visibility and availability of your product offering, such as establishing strategic distribution partnerships with key vendors, and
- investigate product enhancement opportunities to increase the appeal of your product and broaden your customer base in new or emerging markets

See each activity for examples.

Buying trends

In order to assess what customers want, you should first define who your customers are and segment them by type.

For example, in the electronic gaming industry, you could segment consumers by age groups and geography. You could also examine who actually buys the games – young children often have games bought by parents or relatives. You can then target each segment with a specific marketing strategy.

Survey sales and marketing professionals

When surveying sales and marketing professionals, it's important to focus on consumer behavior, needs, and perceptions about your offering, and what kind of marketing and sales strategies are being used.

For instance, how is your organization currently marketing and selling to key customer groups? Have they had notable success with some groups or with certain sales strategies?

Survey distribution channels

Examine your distribution strategies and look for opportunities to increase or enhance your product's visibility.

For example, establishing strategic distribution partnerships with new vendors may open up a number of new retail opportunities – both in-store and online – for your product.

Investigate product enhancement opportunities

Search for innovative ways to enhance your product, such as adding complementary products or services, or rethinking some aspect of the product's design to make it more user friendly.

For example, if your organization sells portable music players, there may be an opportunity to enhance the offering by adding a free membership to an online music service with every player sold.

Question

Which aspects of an analysis of customer groups will have an impact on a business plan?

Options:

1. Examining seasonal and historical customer spending

2. Determining customer ratings of the quality of your product

3. Looking at selling trends of your competitors

4. Surveying sales professionals on their chosen selling pitch

Answer

Option 1: This option is correct. Examining customer spending will help you identify opportunities to create substitutes for competitor products.

Option 2: This option is correct. Investigating product possibilities will help you amend your plan with product enhancements.

Option 3: This option is incorrect. When investigating customer groups, it's important to look at buying trends of customers.

Option 4: This option is incorrect. When surveying sales and marketing professionals, it's important to focus on consumer behavior.

Market analysis: competitors

When conducting business planning, the third area to consider is the competition. First and foremost, you must define who your competitors are. It's easy to become complacent about your competition. Be aware that new competitors emerge quickly – particularly if there are few barriers for new companies entering your industry. You'll also need to assess customer satisfaction with those competitors.

The next step is to evaluate your key competition. You can examine competitors' financial stability, strategy, and success at launching new products or services. For example, if your business plan involves launching a new laptop, you need to know if your competitors have ever done the same thing. If so, were they successful, and why or why not? These details can help refine your business plan and related strategies.

It's also important to assess your competitors' responsiveness to the evolving competitive environment. For example, did any competitors change their strategies immediately after you launched your last product? If so, what did they do? Is it likely they'll take similar steps this time around? And if they do, what steps or actions can you add to your plan to help mitigate this type of competitive pressure?

Focus groups are a good way to identify competitors by asking customers why they prefer certain companies over others. Also, questionnaires that ask customers to rank top competitors are useful to help determine customer preferences and decision-making related to your direct competitors.

Question

Match each market analysis activity to the appropriate type of analysis. Each type of analysis may have more than one match.

Options:

A. Determine what consumers are looking for in a quality service

B. Hold a focus group to determine what your business can do to improve its competitive advantage

C. Investigate the extent of alternative services that your customers use

D. Identify nontraditional entrants into the industry that appeal to your customers

Targets:

1. Customer analysis

2. Competitor analysis

Answer

A customer analysis focuses on what customers are looking for. A focus group can be used to ask them about their wants and needs, to improve your position in the market.

A competitor analysis involves scrutinizing your competition. You can ask customers questions directly about alternative services and nontraditional market entrants to find out why they chose a competitor.

Market analysis: industry

When writing a business plan, you also examine your industry. Industry information is readily available through sources such as government statistics or industry associations. The information can inform you of potential threats to your competitive position. Such threats can include the entry of new competitors, substitute products or services, the bargaining power of customers and suppliers, and the intensity of rivalry.

You should consider several key questions in your industry analysis:

What's the monetary value of your industry in the wider economic and political environment?

What volume of products and services has the industry sold in recent years?

What are the historical trends of the industry?

Have there been other major industry-specific developments relating to technology, price, people, or outsourcing?

Together the different parts of the market analysis will help you develop a business plan or idea that reflects insight about customers, competitors, and industry.

Question
Which market influences might affect your business plan?

Options:
1. Determining what your customers find lacking in your product
2. Your competitors' commercial strength
3. The volume of products an industry has sold in recent years
4. Government foreign trade policy
5. Uncertainty in interest rates

Answer
Option 1: This option is correct. Customer sentiment toward your product or service can affect your business plan.

Option 2: This option is correct. The financial stability and opportunities of your competitors can influence your business plan.

Option 3: This option is correct. The health and success of your industry will have a bearing on the direction of your business plan.

Option 4: This option is incorrect. Although relevant to your business plan, the political environment is considered in the PEST analysis.

Option 5: This option is incorrect. Although an important factor in your business planning, interest rates are considered during the PEST analysis.

x

Learning aid - Examining the External Environment
Scenario planning involves developing potential situations that may be driven by political, economic,

societal, or technological factors. There are four steps in scenario planning:

1. pinpoint the factors of high uncertainty and high impact
2. outline alternative scenarios for those factors
3. select the three most likely scenarios
4. write the scenario descriptions

Factors	Descriptions
Political	Company operations are affected by political factors such as corporate tax, monetary policy, foreign trade policy, competition law, regulation, and government bureaucracy
	Education policy also impacts a business's ability to recruit qualified employees
Economic	Company profitability is influenced by bull or bear markets, infrastructure, inflation, interest rates, fuel prices, and exchange rates
	Some businesses are more prone to business cycle fluctuations than others
Societal	Plans can be affected by societal factors such as the average amount of time people work every week, which typically influences the amount of free time they have
	Consumer spending is often directly related to demographics and social norms
Technological	Company profitability is influenced by technological advances such as the availability of government funding for R&D, investment by competitors into R&D, and new production methods
	Consumer spending and the time it takes for people to buy into technology can impact consumer demand

Learning aid - Market Analysis

Use the table to identify the strengths and weakness in your company. You can print this document, or recreate the table in a word processing or spreadsheet application and use it to complete this activity.

Step	Strengths	Weaknesses
Assess market strategy		
Assess resources		
Evaluate organization and management strategy		
Evaluate financial position		

How a SWOT analysis affects a business

An important step in developing a successful business plan is to identify opportunities and threats. Internal and external analyses yield important information to help you do this. From your internal analysis you'll have considered your company's market strategy, resources, organizational and management strategy, and financial position. Your external analysis will provide possible future scenarios of the political, economic, societal, and technological environment. It will also yield information on customers, competitors, and the industry.

A SWOT analysis is the identification of strengths, weaknesses, opportunities, and threats to your business. Strengths and weaknesses are derived from your internal analysis. Opportunities and threats become apparent during your external analysis.

See each element for examples.

Strengths

Strengths are resources and capabilities that provide a competitive advantage. Examples may include patents on products, your brand in the market, your reputation with customers, a low-cost location, good distribution channels, or reliable infrastructure.

Weaknesses

Weaknesses can be the absence of strengths. For instance, a weakness could be the lack of a patent, a weak brand, a poor reputation, or high operating costs.

Also, something may be both a strength and weakness. For example, having a mature business with a large local presence and skilled workforce can also make you slow to adapt to the changing external environment.

Opportunities

Opportunities are the potential for profit and future growth. Examples include any unfulfilled customer wants or needs, new technological advances, the loosening of regulation, or the removal of barriers to trade.

Threats

Changes in the external environment can present threats. Possible threats could be a change in consumer taste away from your product or service, new substitute products on the market, new regulations that adversely affect your business, or perhaps increased barriers to trade.

You can leverage the information in your SWOT to build on your strengths, deal with any weaknesses, capitalize on opportunities, and reduce vulnerability to threats.

You'll then be in a position to see your business plan in context, and maximize your competitive advantage by matching your company's resources to its environment.

A SWOT analysis should be a simple strategic review that you can do quickly. It's an important aspect of your business plan in the context of your company's internal and external environment. You can then present it as a key addition to your business plan.

Make your SWOT analysis a creative process. Prompt a robust debate among your management team or investors. The SWOT analysis shouldn't be too structured or limited. Instead, it should be allowed to evolve.

Collectively addressing perceived weaknesses and threats will add value to your business plan and make it more resilient to its changing environment.

Question

Consider Mike, a product manager for a multinational clothing chain. He's just completed a SWOT analysis for a new line of clothes he's proposing to market to men.

Match each item from his SWOT analysis to the relevant category.

Options:

A. A team of skilled fashion designers
B. High staff turnover
C. A growing economy
D. Higher sales tax on clothing

Targets:

1. Strength
2. Weakness
3. Opportunity
4. Threat

Answer

Strengths are internal to the organization. A skilled workforce is an example of a strength to any organization.

Weaknesses are internal to the organization. High staff turnover is a weaknesses for most organizations – especially a highly skilled workforce.

Opportunities are external to the organization. A growing economy is a good opportunity for the retail market.

Threats are external to the organization. Higher sales tax on clothing is a threat to the profit margins of retail organizations.

Conducting a SWOT analysis

You begin your SWOT analysis by listing important opportunities and threats in the context of your company's strengths and weaknesses. You should also keep in mind the strategic objectives of your business plan. For ease of discussion, you can then rank the factors in order of importance and assign a weight or importance score to each factor. Focus on the most relevant factors and present them neatly on a one-page chart

Reflect

How do you think you can use a SWOT to maximize competitive advantage? Write down your response or enter it in a text file in your word-processor application (or in a text editor such as Notepad) and save it to your hard drive for later viewing.

You may have noted that to maximize competitive advantage, you must put customer needs first. You can do this by being aware of your customers' needs when conducting a SWOT.

You can then prioritize and address any weaknesses in meeting their needs. Your market analysis is therefore very important in your SWOT analysis.

To focus on your customer's needs, determine the relevance of your strengths and weaknesses to meeting their needs. A strength is only relevant if you can exploit it as an opportunity or use it to overcome potential threats. Conversely, a weakness is only relevant if it's a threat to the success of your business.

For example, new technology identified in your PEST analysis can be either a threat or an opportunity depending on your company's ability to capitalize on the technology.

Statements should be short, but detailed. For example, a strength could be "our market share is 30% compared with our nearest rival's 20%." If further detail is required you can attach an appendix.

Consider Guarded World, a company supplying solar panels across Europe. Beth, a manager at Guarded World, is doing a SWOT analysis to refine her business plan. She notes the biggest strength for Guarded World is that it offers sustainable, renewable, and environmentally friendly energy. This clearly differentiates it from companies offering traditional fossil fuels. The weakness of solar power is the high setup costs for potential customers. Also, it's hard to capture enough solar energy in some countries.

Opportunities for growth exist in the solar industry because oil, coal, and gas are finite resources. As supply of these resources diminishes and demand increases, the price of fossil fuels will increase. As prices rise in the traditional fuel industries, there's potential for Guarded World to compete on price. Threats to the solar industry include other renewable energy sources such as wind power.

Question

What factors are important in conducting a SWOT analysis?

Options:

1. Identifying important opportunities and threats in the context of your company's strengths and weaknesses
2. Ranking the factors in order of importance and assigning a weight to each factor
3. Ranking the factors in the order of strengths, weaknesses, opportunities, threats
4. Identifying important weaknesses in the context of your company's strengths and opportunities

Answer

Option 1: This option is correct. A SWOT analysis requires identifying important opportunities and threats in the external environment. These should be in context of your company's strengths and weaknesses.

Option 2: This option is correct. A SWOT analysis requires you to rank factors in order of importance and weight them. This allows you to prioritize your strategies.

Option 3: This option is incorrect. Ranking must be done in order of importance for each strength, weakness, opportunity, and threat.

Option 4: This option is incorrect. A SWOT analysis identifies important opportunities and threats in the context of your company's strengths and weaknesses.

Using a SWOT for your business plan

A SWOT analysis is a glimpse at your company's competitive position and can be used to generate possible strategies for your business plan. It gives management an overview of possibilities and problems affecting the business. In addressing opportunities and threats, your business plan will become more credible and robust. A good SWOT analysis gives credence to your business plan because it shows how prepared the business is for the future.

Using your SWOT analysis information involves more than simply taking advantage of opportunities and minimizing threats. It may in fact be best to improve competitive advantage by finding a "best fit" between strengths and opportunities. You may have to prioritize business planning strategies – for instance, overcoming a weakness before being able to follow an opportunity.

You can organize your strategies into the SWOT matrix. Strength-opportunity strategies pursue opportunities that are a good fit to the company's strengths. Weakness-opportunity strategies overcome weaknesses to pursue opportunities in your external environment. Strength-threat strategies identify ways to use strengths to reduce any vulnerability to external threats. Weakness-threat strategies establish a defensive plan to prevent weaknesses from making your company vulnerable to external threats. Once you've identified your various strategies you can prioritize them to maximize competitive advantage.

See each strategy for an example.

Strength-Opportunity strategies

A strength-opportunity strategy could be to increase advertising to highlight your existing sales record given low advertising costs.

Weakness-Opportunity strategies

A weakness-opportunity strategy could be to diversify into a new market given the decrease in demand for your product.

Strength-Threat strategies

A strength-threat strategy could be to acquire a failing competitor given your high revenue and the growing demand for your products.

Weakness-Threat strategies

A weakness-threat strategy could be to downsize your business due to falling demand for your product in an economic downturn.

Remember Beth? She is doing a SWOT analysis for Guarded World, a company that supplies solar panels. One of Guarded World's strengths is a sustainable, renewable, and environmentally friendly source of energy.

As part of a strength-opportunity strategy, she decides to use this strength as a unique selling point to take advantage of the growth possibilities in the solar industry.

As part of a strength-threat strategy, Beth will increase advertising to promote Guarded World's strengths over the potential competition from wind powered energy.

However, Beth is concerned about the high setup costs for potential customers. Also she knows it can be hard to capture large enough quantities of solar energy. Her industry analysis also indicated the emergence of a new competitor specializing in wind power.

Beth prioritizes a weakness-threat strategy. She decides to investigate technological advances that could perhaps lower the current cost to customers.

As a weakness-opportunity strategy she decides to investigate the possibilities of acquiring a company that specializes in wind power.

Question

Consider Lara, she's a development manager in a multinational organization, Blazerfire. She's building a business plan to determine the viability of a new electronic game for a client. Access the learning aid Blazerfire's SWOT for further information.

How does Blazerfire's SWOT analysis affect Lara's business plan?

Options:

1. Lara's business plan needs to describe how to use multiple revenue streams to exploit rising client marketing budgets

2. The plan should show how to address the company's low return on investment given the potential for clients to develop games in-house

3. The plan needs to describe how to capitalize on the company's low employee turnover to off-set the threat of the client developing in-house

4. The plan needs to show how to use low overheads to convince her client that an aging work force won't affect its ability to develop a video game

5. The plan needs to describe how to use multiple revenue streams to exploit the company's rising tax liability

Answer

Option 1: This option is correct. This is a strength-opportunity strategy. Lara should use her company's internal strengths such as multiple revenue streams to exploit external opportunities.

Option 2: This option is correct. This is a weakness-threat strategy. This would be a top priority for Lara as the client may be able to develop the game cheaper on its own.

Option 3: This option is correct. This is a strength-threat strategy. Low employee turnover means there's a lot of expertise in Lara's company. She could perhaps describe in her plan how to use this information to offset the client's lack of marketing skills.

Option 4: This option is incorrect. Strategies built on a company's strengths should be used to offset opportunities or threats, not weaknesses.

Option 5: This option is incorrect. Lara should use her company's internal strengths such as multiple revenue streams to exploit external opportunities. Tax liabilities are a threat.

Learning aid - **Blazerfire's SWOT**

Use Blazerfire's SWOT to determine how the analysis will affect the business plan.

Strengths	Weaknesses	Opportunities	Threats
Low employee turnover	Aging employee base	Rising marketing budgets	Change in tax legislation
Low overheads	Low return on investment	New advertising mediums	Ability of clients to self-market at a low cost
Multiple revenue streams	High production costs		

Learning aid - **SWOT Analysis**

Use this table to identify the strengths, weaknesses, opportunities, and threats in your company. You can print this document, or recreate the table in a word processing or spreadsheet application and use it to complete this activity.

	Strengths	Weaknesses
Opportunities		
Threats		

CHAPTER THREE

Preparing for Implementation

The connection between planning, implementation, and control
Implementing a business plan

Many managers are involved in creating business plans in their organizations. A business plan outlines a set of business goals and how those goals can be achieved. Once a business plan has been created and communicated, it needs to be implemented. It also needs to be continuously reviewed and controlled to ensure it's being carried out effectively.

A business plan generally contains high-level operational plans and strategies, and makes general financial forecasts. An implementation plan, on the other hand, goes into more detail. For example, it usually includes detailed organizational information such as organization charts and job descriptions, as well as procedures and manuals. It also includes detailed operational budgets.

The planning, implementation, and subsequent control phases of a business plan shouldn't be regarded as separate functions that operate independently. Instead they should be integrated into the organization's overall activities and viewed as part of a continuous strategic process.

The planning stage is the first part of the process. At this stage, you develop your business plan. The plan should clearly state what needs to be accomplished. It should also provide general information about how this should be done.

Implementation is the next part of the process. At this stage, you put the plan into action. This involves devising and managing action plans and establishing accountability among employees. You also need to ensure resources are available and aligned with the plan's goals and objectives in order to successfully realize the plan.

No matter how well a plan is constructed, it needs to be reviewed from time to time. At the third stage of the process – the control stage – you assess how effectively the plan is being implemented. This allows you to measure the performance of employees and processes, and modify and enhance your action plan if necessary.

Establishing a direct link from planning to implementation to control will help you implement your business plan more successfully.

When these functions operate in a unified, interdependent way, your business plan is more likely to support the organization's goals and objectives.

Question

Which statement correctly describes the relationship between planning, implementation, and control?

Options:
1. The elements operate interdependently and form part of a continuous strategic process
2. Each element is a separate function that operates independently
3. Implementation and control are linked, but planning is an independent function

Answer

Option 1: This is the correct option. Planning, implementation, and control should operate interdependently. They form a continuous cycle and are fundamentally linked.

Option 2: This option is incorrect. Planning, implementation, and control shouldn't operate independently from each other. Each element should be viewed as part of a continuous strategic planning process.

Option 3: This option is incorrect. All three elements are linked and should be integrated into an organization's overall activities.

Facing challenges

When it comes to implementing your business plan, you'll want to carry out the process in a smooth, effective way. However, you may encounter difficulties during implementation. It's important to overcome such challenges when they occur and get your plan back on track as quickly as possible.

Next, you'll observe an interaction involving Chang, who's just implemented a business plan to increase sales in his organization. He talks to his colleague, Betty, about some of the setbacks he experienced along the way.

Follow along as Chang discusses the implementation phase of his business plan with Betty and describes some of the challenges he faced.

Chang: It was tough. Some of the team didn't want to make any changes at all. Complaining that we don't have enough people on the ground to actually increase sales.

Chang is a little stressed.

Betty: How did you deal with it?

Betty is interested.

Chang: Well, I said we should use the people we have more effectively, without overloading anybody. Shift our focus to new territories instead of concentrating on established ones...and make adjustments along the way.

Chang is determined.

Betty: Smart! Bet it wasn't easy getting buy-in from everyone...

Betty is engaged.

Chang: It wasn't. But when the team understood exactly what they had to do – and why – it was easier. Ran like clockwork after that.

Chang is relieved.

Betty: So it all worked out?

Betty is pleased.

Chang: Seems so! And the best part? I'm getting more respect from the team and I feel more confident – it's win-win!

Chang is happy.

Question

What benefits do you think Chang gains by being able to implement his business plan effectively?

Options:

1. He's able to get the team to focus on how to best make the new sales strategy work
2. He manages to overcome barriers that could cause his plan to fail
3. He enhances his credibility among his team members
4. He feels more confident about his management skills
5. He's able to disguise the fact that he doesn't have a clear action plan 6. He won't have to monitor and control future business plans as closely

Answer

Option 1: This option is correct. By communicating clearly to his team members and working to overcome their initial resistance, Chang is able to introduce his business plan smoothly and efficiently.

Option 2: This option is correct. Employee resistance and poor communication are just two of the many reasons why business plans fail. Chang is able to avoid these causes of failure and successfully implement his business plan.

Option 3: This option is correct. By successfully implementing his business plan, Chang gains credibility among his employees.

Option 4: This option is correct. By implementing his business plan successfully, Chang feels more confident as a manager.

Option 5: This option is incorrect. It's unlikely that Chang would be able to implement a business plan successfully without drawing up a number of detailed action plans first.

Option 6: This option is incorrect. Successfully implementing one business plan doesn't mean that Chang won't have to review and control future plans just as closely.

Benefits of effective implementation

As a manager, you'll be able to gain real benefits by implementing your business plans successfully. For one thing, you'll be able to introduce your strategies and ideas smoothly, causing a minimum amount of disruption to your employees. Your team can then focus on making the necessary changes and on reconciling new and emerging strategies with existing ones.

By implementing a business plan effectively, you overcome the reasons why many plans fail. Typical reasons include employee resistance due to pessimism, skepticism, or a general unwillingness to do things differently. Inadequate resources, IT constraints, and poor communication are other reasons why plans fail.

When you successfully implement an idea or strategy, it's likely that you'll gain credibility among your employees. For example, they may feel you now have greater legitimacy as a manager. This could enhance your reputation and overall standing within the organization.

Successfully implementing a business plan may also make you feel more confident as a manager. And your organization as a whole can benefit too. Through the implementation process, employees will have acquired more knowledge and experience, meaning the company is better positioned to adapt to future changes.

Coordinating the process

To implement a business plan successfully, you need to coordinate and manage all implementation- related activities in an effective way. You also need to promote implementation-centered behavior, decision making, and problem solving among your employees.

There are a number of steps you can take to coordinate the implementation phase of your business plan. To begin, you develop action plans that outline the tasks that need to be completed. Next you ensure that implementation can be supported in your organization. You create a reporting system to help you monitor progress. It's also important to be able to control and modify your plans. Finally, you need to assess the outcomes.

See each step to learn more about it.

1. Develop action plans

You should develop action plans to help you implement your business plan. An action plan is a series of tasks that need to be completed in order to accomplish a particular business plan objective, or set of objectives. It also sets out the time frame for performing those tasks and the sequence in which they should be performed.

Action plans identify the unit or department that has overall responsibility for accomplishing the necessary tasks. They also provide a basis for allocating resources, such as people, time, and money.

2. Ensure implementation can be supported

Implementation efforts need to be supported throughout the organization if they're to be successful. So it's important to ensure the appropriate organizational infrastructure is in place to provide this support.

This might involve reallocating resources to make sure you have sufficient employees with the right mix of skills to achieve your goals. It may also involve realigning individual responsibilities so your team members know exactly what they're accountable for. It might even be necessary to restructure a department or division, and its policies and procedures, to ensure strategies and plans can be implemented more efficiently.

3. Create a reporting system

It's important to create an effective management reporting system. This should help you measure the performance of employees and the results they've achieved to date, and take corrective actions if necessary.

Whatever reporting system you use, you should be confident in the accuracy of the information reported. You should also ensure the relevant information is reported at appropriate intervals – for example daily, weekly, monthly, or quarterly – and on a timely basis.

4. Control and modify plans

During the implementation phase, plans frequently stray off course. So when implementing a plan, you need to have clear procedures in place for controlling and modifying objectives, strategies, and action plans when necessary.

You must act quickly and decisively when problems are identified – if the corrective action is delayed, the problem can become more complex and take longer to solve. Focus on pinpointing the cause of each problem, revising your plans, and developing corrective actions. Then implement the corrective strategy immediately.

5. Assess outcomes

When your plan has been developed, implemented, and controlled, it's important to evaluate the results of your efforts. The main purpose of this evaluation is to provide information that will be useful in developing future business plans. It should be broad in scope, and should identify strengths as well as weaknesses. It should also identify the reasons for the success or failure of different parts of the plan.

This process should help you find out whether strategic goals have actually been achieved. It should also help you assess whether things are better or worse in your organization as a result of the implemented changes.

Implementation often receives less focus and attention than the actual development of a business plan. This is a mistake – effective implementation of the strategies and ideas contained in the plan is a very important activity. By following these steps, you'll be able to coordinate the implementation of your business plans more effectively. And you'll have the best chance of implementing your ideas and strategies smoothly.

Question

Which steps should you take to coordinate the implementation of a business plan?

Options:

1. Compile a series of tasks that need to be completed in order to accomplish the plan's objectives

2. Move extra resources onto your team and realign individual responsibilities within the organization

3. Ensure you receive accurate weekly reports and take corrective action when problems are identified

4. Evaluate the implementation program by examining what went wrong and what succeeded

5. Eliminate all uncertainty from the business plan to avoid having to modify your strategies later

6. Only consider implementation procedures that fit in with your organization's existing way of doing things

Answer

Option 1: This option is correct. You should develop action plans to help you implement your business plan. An action plan sets out the tasks to be completed, the time frame for performing those tasks, and the sequence in which they should be performed.

Option 2: This option is correct. Implementation efforts need to be supported throughout the organization if they're to be successful. This may involve reallocating resources and realigning responsibilities.

Option 3: This option is correct. It's important to create an effective management reporting system. When problems are reported, you can then focus on revising your plans and implementing corrective actions.

Option 4: This option is correct. When your plan has been developed, implemented, and controlled, it's important to evaluate the results of your efforts. This evaluation should be broad in scope, and should identify strengths as well as weaknesses.

Option 5: This option is incorrect. A significant amount of uncertainty is associated with every business plan. Rather than trying to eliminate uncertainty altogether, you should develop procedures that allow you to modify your plan when problems arise.

Option 6: This option is incorrect. To implement your plans more efficiently, it might be necessary to restructure the organization and its policies and procedures.

Learning aid - Coordinating Implementation Activities

You can follow a number of steps to help you coordinate the implementation phase of a business plan.

Step	Further details
1: Develop action plans	An action plan • describes the tasks that need to be completed in order to accomplish a particular business plan objective, or set of objectives • sets out the time frame for performing tasks • lists the sequence in which tasks should be performed • identifies the unit or department that has overall responsibility for accomplishing the necessary tasks, and • provides a basis for allocating resources, such as people, time, and money
2: Ensure implementation can be supported	Ensure the appropriate organizational infrastructure is in place to provide support during the implementation phase by • reallocating resources as necessary • realigning individual responsibilities, and • restructuring a department or division – and its policies and procedures – to help ensure strategies and plans can be implemented more efficiently
3: Create a reporting system	An effective management reporting system • allows you to measure the performance of employees and the results they've achieved to date • allows you to take corrective actions if necessary • provides accurate information, and • reports information at appropriate intervals and on a timely basis
4: Control and modify plans	Having clear procedures in place for modifying strategies and action plans when necessary • allows you to act quickly and decisively when problems are identified • helps you focus on pinpointing the cause of each problem and developing corrective actions • allows you to implement the corrective strategy immediately
5: Assess outcomes	A thorough evaluation of your plan • provides information that will be useful in developing future business plans • is broad in scope • identifies strengths as well as weaknesses • identifies the reasons for the success or failure of different parts of the plan • helps you find out whether strategic goals have actually been achieved, and • helps you assess whether things are better or worse in your organization as a result of the implemented changes

Planning to facilitate the implementation of a business plan

Action plans

Without careful action planning, the strategies you'd like to implement in your organization are unlikely to become reality. So when coordinating the implementation phase of a business plan, the first step is to develop targeted action plans. An action plan is a series of tasks that need to be completed in order to accomplish a particular objective.

The objectives an action plan aims to accomplish should always be linked to the objectives set out in the business plan itself. Formulate these objectives after a thorough analysis of the organization has taken place. Your action plan should describe how to accomplish these objectives in the short term – most action plans cover periods of one year or less.

Before creating an action plan, it's important to list the tactical objectives you want to achieve over the action-planning period. To do this, you should review the long-term strategic direction the organization is taking. For example, one of the organization's long-term objectives might be to cut operating costs across the entire organization by 10% next year. Your tactical objectives should be in line with this.

You should also review the environment the organization is operating in. This involves taking internal strengths and weaknesses, and external threats and opportunities, into consideration. For example, maybe the organization is operating in a downturn economy.

For your objectives to be realistic, you'll probably have to make assumptions about future conditions and trends. For example, you might make assumptions about consumer spending, technological breakthroughs, or the arrival of new competitors.

Your tactical objectives should include primary financial objectives. These are likely to relate to current and expected sales, revenues, and return on investment.

You should also create functional objectives, which are related to your products. Functional objectives might cover areas such as quality, development, pricing, and packaging.

Finally, it's important to create non-product objectives too. These objectives tend to relate to the support functions within your organization. These areas include manufacturing, market research, training, and human resource development.

Question

Which statement is correct?

Options:

1. Most action plans are short term in focus and cover a 12-month period or less

2. Most action plans are medium term in focus and cover a period of one to three years

3. Most action plans are long term in focus and cover a period of three to five years

Answer

Option 1: This is the correct option. Most action plans cover periods of one year or less. So an action plan should describe how to implement strategies in the short term.

Option 2: This option is incorrect. Most action plans are short term in focus. They usually describe how to implement plans and ideas in 12 months or less.

Option 3: This option is incorrect. Whereas strategic business planning has a long-term focus, action planning is concerned with implementing strategies in 12 months or less.

Content of action plans

Some organizations undertake action planning at the same time as strategic business planning. This is usually a mistake. Business planning involves considering the bigger picture. But with action planning, you're focusing on the detail. So it's usually better to do action planning afterwards.

Action plans typically contain information on a number of different areas. For example, an action plan usually describes the roles and responsibilities of teams and individuals during the implementation process. It lists expected results, along with specific goals and milestones. It outlines specific action steps that need to be taken. It also provides schedules and sets out resource requirements.

See each area to learn more about it.

Roles and responsibilities

It's important to make sure that your team members understand their individual roles and responsibilities in the implementation process. They need to know exactly what's expected of them and what they're required to do.

Expected results

A typical action plan clearly states the goals and objectives the plan aims to achieve. It also describes the expected results – or outcomes.

Specific action steps

It's important to break the work involved in your action plan down into specific action steps or activities. When you've listed the necessary activities, you can then sequence them in a logical order.

Schedules

It helps to provide detailed schedules for each project and subproject. Schedules show how long each activity is expected to take – and when it should take place.

Resource requirements

An action plan should set out the resources you need to successfully implement your strategies and ideas. The main resources you need to carry out an action plan are people, time, space, and equipment.

Question

Which of the following elements does an action plan typically contain?

Options:

1. A detailed executive summary for senior management
2. A list of the goals you expect to achieve by implementing your plan
3. An overview of the strategic direction the organization is taking
4. The number of people needed to implement your plan, and a description of each person's role
5. A schedule showing exactly when each activity is to take place
6. A list of all the steps necessary to achieve your desired results

Answer

Option 1: This option is incorrect. It's not necessary to include an executive summary in an action plan. Action plans should focus on the detail of how to implement your business plan.

Option 2: This option is correct. A typical action plan clearly states the goals and objectives the plan aims to achieve.

Option 3: This option is incorrect. Action plans shouldn't include high-level strategic information. Instead, they should set out exactly how to achieve your desired results.

Option 4: This option is correct. An action plan should outline the resources you need to successfully implement your strategies and ideas. Individual roles and responsibilities should also be described.

Option 5: This option is correct. Action plans should include detailed schedules. Schedules show how long each activity is expected to take – and when it should take place.

Option 6: This option is correct. The work involved in your action plan should be broken down into specific action steps or activities. And they should be sequenced in a logical order.

Action planning steps 1 to 3

You can follow seven steps to help you create the main sections of an action plan. First, clarify the outcomes you want to achieve. For each outcome, list the activities necessary to achieve it. Then put the activities in order. The fourth step is to assign responsibilities for completing each activity among your employees. Then determine the resources you need to implement your plan. And determine the likely costs of implementing it. Finally, create a schedule showing the timelines involved.

When clarifying the outcomes you want to achieve, you describe the expected results of the various activities in your plan.

For example, imagine your department has a plan to develop a new software product. When devising an action plan to achieve this goal, you could state that your desired outcomes are to have a prototype ready for testing within six months; and to launch the new product within a year.

The second step to take when creating an action plan is to list the activities necessary to achieve each outcome. It's a good idea to get the relevant teams involved in brainstorming the activities. Each activity should be clearly written, to avoid confusion and misinterpretation later.

For example, if the desired outcome is to have a software prototype ready for testing within six months, you need to complete a number of activities. These might include designing an initial version of the prototype and then revising and enhancing that prototype.

Reviewing the prototype and providing feedback on any additions or changes that might be necessary are other possible activities. It's probably also important to identify basic user requirements.

The third step is to put the activities in a logical order, so you tackle them in the correct sequence. In this example, the first activity undertaken should be to identify basic user requirements. Then you can design an initial prototype. After that, you review it and provide feedback on any additions or changes that are necessary. The final activity is to revise and enhance the prototype.

Question

Kevin is a manager in an insurance company. He's proposing a new business plan to help the company strengthen its web presence. His plan involves developing a range of innovative online services over the next 12 months.

How should Kevin use action planning to facilitate the implementation of his business plan?

Options:

1. State that one of the main outcomes he wants to achieve is to make the web site more user friendly

2. Write down all the activities his team needs to undertake to make the web site more appealing

3. List the task of uploading up-to-date content to the web site before the task of carrying out quality control checks

4. Give employees the freedom to work out for themselves how to achieve the desired results

5. Present his business idea to key decision makers to get financial approval for his plan

Answer

Option 1: This option is correct. Kevin's first step should be to clarify the outcomes he wants to achieve by his action plan. Outcomes are the expected results of the various activities in a plan.

Option 2: This option is correct. The second step Kevin should take is to list the activities necessary to achieve each outcome. Each activity should be clearly written, to avoid confusion and misinterpretation later.

Option 3: This option is correct. The third step Kevin needs to take is to put the activities in a logical order. In this way, his team can tackle each activity in the correct sequence.

Option 4: This option is incorrect. Kevin should list the specific activities that are necessary to achieve each of his desired outcomes.

Option 5: This option is incorrect. While it's important that Kevin's plan has been approved financially, he should have the necessary approval before he starts action planning.

Action planning steps 4 to 7

When creating an action plan, the fourth step is to assign responsibilities for completing each activity among your team members. Unless you specifically assign responsibility for carrying out a task, it probably won't get done. So your action plan should make it clear who has responsibility – and authority – for ensuring that each activity is completed. You should also identify the individuals, groups, or units who are involved in carrying out each activity.

Consider again the activities you examined earlier – they're listed in the first column of this table. In the second column, responsibility for each activity is allocated to a specific employee with adequate skills and experience. This person has overall responsibility for getting the task done. This person also has the authority to make any necessary decisions relating to the task. In the third column, the individuals, teams, and groups involved in the task are identified.

Reflect

The fifth step you should take when creating an action plan is to determine the resources you need to implement your plan.

Write down your response or enter it in a text file in your word-processor application (or in a text editor such as Notepad) and save it to your hard drive for later viewing.

You may have noted that it's crucial to factor in enough people and support services from the outset to implement your action plan effectively. Inadequate resources can cause your plan to fall behind schedule – or to fail. But almost any problem can be solved with adequate resources.

Always try to avoid underestimating the resources you need. If projects don't run smoothly, you may need to draw on extra backup in the future. And always ensure the employees you request have the skills necessary to get the job done.

Try to list the specific resources required to complete each of the activities in your plan. For example, you could decide you need six designers and ten programmers to design the initial software prototype. And you may decide you require half these resources – three designers and five programmers – to revise and enhance it.

The sixth step is to determine the specific costs required to implement your action plan. To work this out, you need to carefully examine each activity in your plan.

Try to estimate the cost of the human resources you require to get each activity done, along with the costs of materials, services, transportation – and any other costs you're likely to incur. You can then incorporate the specific cost of each activity into an overall budget for your action plan.

For example, if you consider the activity of designing an initial prototype, you'll have to factor in the time of six designers and ten programmers. You'll also have to factor in other costs related to that activity, such as a computer upgrade. Then you can estimate the total cost for the activity as a whole.

When creating an action plan, the seventh and final step is to create a schedule that outlines the time frame when each activity should take place. The schedule should provide key milestones, such as the start date and completion date for all activities.

When you've scheduled each activity, you need to ensure that your schedule makes sense. There should be no conflicts or overlaps in your time line. And each activity should be scheduled in the correct order.

In the previous example, the first activity – identifying user requirements – could be scheduled to take place in January. The initial design phase of the prototype could span the months of February, March, and April. The prototype could be reviewed during the first half of May, with feedback provided in the third week of that month. Finally, the prototype could be revised from the fourth week in May to the end of June.

Action planning should guide the day-to-day activities of your organization. By following these seven steps, you'll be able to create effective action plans that convert your ideas and strategies into action. This should help you achieve your own objectives as a manager – as well as your organization's long-term goals.

Question

Kevin is still trying to implement a new strategy to strengthen his organization's web presence. His strategy involves developing a range of innovative online services over the next 12 months.

Sequence the examples of what Kevin needs to do to use action planning appropriately to facilitate the implementation of his business plan.

Options:

A. Assign responsibility for designing the look and feel of the web site to a specific person

B. Determine that a team of three programmers and four designers is required

C. Determine the cost of using three programmers and four designers for the duration of the project

D. Create a schedule that shows the start date and end date for each activity

Answer

Correct answer(s):

Assign responsibility for designing the look and feel of the web site to a specific person is ranked The first step in this sequence

Kevin needs to assign responsibility for completing each activity before he undertakes any of the other steps. Unless responsibility for carrying out a task is specifically allocated, the task probably won't get done.

Determine that a team of three programmers and four designers is required is ranked The second step in this sequence

Kevin should determine the resources he needs after he's assigned responsibilities. He should determine the likely costs and create a schedule afterwards.

Determine the cost of using three programmers and four designers for the duration of the project is ranked The third step in this sequence

Kevin should assign responsibilities and determine the resources he needs before determining cost. Finally, he should create a schedule.

Create a schedule that shows the start date and end date for each activity is ranked The fourth step in this sequence

Creating a schedule that outlines the time frame when each activity takes place should be the final step Kevin takes to implement his action plan. Before that, he should assign responsibilities, determine the resources required, and the costs involved.

Supporting implementation

After developing an action plan, it's important to ensure you can actually implement it. To do this, you should ensure the current organizational infrastructure can support the plan. For example, you might find it beneficial to ask for a reallocation of certain departmental resources or a realignment of certain responsibilities. It's also a good idea to relate rewards to results wherever possible and to conduct a review of your internal procedures and policies.

Building support for your plan might require a reallocation of certain departmental resources within your department or division – or proposing a different approach to how resources are used. For example, you could suggest that some key employees are "shared" by a number of functional managers, so they can work across several projects simultaneously. The goal is to ensure you have the right number of people, with the appropriate skills, to complete the activities set out in your action plan.

Ensuring there is adequate support to implement your plan might also involve realigning individual responsibilities. To do this, you need to make specific employees accountable for each activity in your action plan.

For example, if you're testing a new product, you should make it clear who is accountable for each stage of the process – from drawing up quality control checklists to notifying the relevant people of the results.

You should also consider relating rewards to results. When people know what types of rewards they can expect for successfully implementing your strategies, you may find it easier to manage and direct their behavior.

So try to link key result areas of your action plan to specific performance bonuses or awards. For example, if one of your desired outcomes is to increase sales, you could tell your sales team that anyone who exceeds targets by 25% or more will receive a financial reward at the end of the year.

To build support for the implementation process, you can also consider conducting a review of your internal procedures and policies. Your action plan may require new ways of doing things. So it's essential that internal processes can be revised and adjusted accordingly. For example, reducing the number of people involved in a review cycle or purchasing materials from a different supplier may help you implement your strategies more effectively.

Question

Imagine your department has developed a business plan to grow sales by 15% over the next 12 months.

How could you build support for implementing this plan?

Options:

1. Move key personnel from the administration team to the sales team

2. Ensure all salespeople know exactly how many leads they need to generate each week

3. State that people who exceed sales targets are eligible for the "Salesperson of the Year" award

4. Change an internal procedure so sales reports are generated electronically, instead of manually

5. Ensure everyone in the organization continues to work in tried-and-tested ways

6. Avoid making any commitment about the awarding of bonuses at the end of the project

Answer

Option 1: This option is correct. You may need to reallocate resources to ensure you have the right number of people, with the appropriate skills, to complete the activities set out in your plan.

Option 2: This option is correct. To build support, you may need to realign responsibilities and make specific employees accountable for each activity in your action plan.

Option 3: This option is correct. You can relate rewards to results by linking key result areas of your action plan to specific performance bonuses or awards.

Option 4: This option is correct. To build support, you should conduct a review of your internal procedures and policies. Your action plan may require new ways of doing things.

Option 5: This option is incorrect. Revising your organization's internal procedures and policies may help you implement your action plan more effectively. So always examine new ways of doing things.

Option 6: This option is incorrect. You should be clear about any rewards that are available. When people know what types of rewards they can expect for successfully implementing your strategies, it can be easier to direct their behavior.

x

Learning aids - Action Planning Steps

You can follow seven steps to help you create the main sections of an action plan.

Step	Details
1: Clarify outcomes	• Clarify the outcomes you want to achieve in your action plan. • Outcomes are the expected results of the various activities in your plan.
2: List activities	• List the activities necessary to achieve each outcome. • Get the relevant teams involved in brainstorming the activities. • Each activity should be clearly written, to avoid confusion and misinterpretation later.
3: Put activities in order	• Put the activities in a logical order. • Tackle each activity in the correct sequence.
4: Assign responsibilities	• Assign responsibilities for completing each activity among your team members. • Make it clear who has responsibility – and authority – for ensuring that each activity is completed. • Identify the individuals, groups, or units who are involved in carrying out each activity.
5: Determine resources	• Factor in enough people and support services from the outset to implement your action plan effectively. • Avoid underestimating the resources you need. • Ensure the employees you request have the skills necessary to get the job done. • List the specific resources required to complete each of the activities in your plan.
6: Determine costs	• Determine the specific costs required to implement your action plan. • To determine costs, examine each activity in your plan. • Estimate the cost of the human resources you require to get each activity done. • Estimate the costs of materials, services, and transportation – and any other costs you're likely to incur. • Incorporate the cost of each activity into an overall budget for your action plan.
7: Create a schedule	• Create a schedule that outlines the time frame when each activity should take place. • The schedule should provide key milestones, such as the start date and completion date for all activities. • Ensure your schedule makes sense. • Ensure each activity is scheduled in the correct order.

Creating a reporting structure that facilitates the implementation

Creating a reporting system

After you've developed an action plan – and ensured its implementation can be supported in your organization – you need to determine how your business plan can be measured and controlled. You can create a management reporting system to help you do this. A proper reporting system can help you monitor progress in relation to targets and outcomes. And it can confirm whether or not your business plan is on track.

When you establish a reporting system, you'll be able to measure how your team is performing – and quantify the results. If the results aren't satisfactory, you can take corrective action if necessary. To create a reporting system, you need to define key performance indicators – and set parameters for each one. It's also necessary to relate performance measures to employee behavior and use comparative data to identify trends. Finally, it's important to structure report formats effectively.

To create a reporting system, you first need to define key performance measurement areas – or indicators – in your organization. These areas should be critical to your organization's success. It should be possible to measure and report each one.

And it's important to identify a good mix of performance areas. However, avoid choosing too many – otherwise, your reporting system will be too complicated. So try to limit yourself to four or five main areas, such as customer service, internal operations, innovation and development, and financial performance.

Key performance indicators based on these areas could include the level of customer satisfaction reported, the number of new technologies adopted, the number of new products developed, and the level of operating cash flow.

After you've defined key performance indicators, you need to set performance levels – or parameters – for each one. In other words, establish acceptable levels of performance for the indicators identified.

To set performance levels, you can establish benchmarks or targets for employees to meet. Targets usually relate to quality, time, and cost – and they must be realistic. For example, you could set a quality-related target by stating that 99.8% of the products you produce should be defect-free when shipped.

You could set a time-related target by announcing that new products must be brought to market within eight months. And you could set a cost-related target by stating that production costs can't exceed $2,000,000. If your targets aren't met, you need to act immediately.

Question

A key performance indicator in many organizations is the level of customer complaints.

What parameters do you think you should set for this indicator?

Options:

1. The number of customer complaints received must not exceed 25 per week

2. The organization must never receive any customer complaints

3. Employees must do everything in their power to reduce the number of customer complaints received

Answer

Option 1: This is the correct option. An acceptable level of performance for the indicator has been established. As long as the number of customer complaints doesn't exceed 25 per week, management won't be concerned about performance in this area.

Option 2: This option is incorrect. The target of receiving zero customer complaints isn't realistic. Managers should always set realistic parameters.

Option 3: This option is incorrect. While the statement is undoubtedly true, the level of customer complaints that's deemed to be acceptable isn't provided. And it doesn't provide any benchmark or target for employees to work toward.

To create a reporting system, the next step is to relate performance measures to actual employee behavior. To do this, you should incorporate the various performance targets you've identified into specific work plans and job descriptions. This should help encourage employees to meet – or exceed – acceptable performance levels.

It's a good idea to offer employees rewards and recognition when they've achieved performance targets. This can help you get the results you desire from your team members. It can also inspire and motivate them to continue doing excellent work.

For example, you could tell team members that if they increase productivity by the required target of 20%, they'll each receive a bonus. You could also congratulate an employee who resolves customer queries within a certain target time with gift certificates or additional vacation time.

When creating a reporting system, the next thing to do is to use comparative data to identify significant trends and relationships. This can help you determine how the current performance of your employees is likely to impact the future operations of the business.

One common way of comparing data is to analyze trends over time. Another method is to examine the performance of different organizations or projects using the same key performance indicators. This can help you predict whether your project is likely to succeed – and whether any issues are likely to arise.

For example, you could use benchmarks from successful projects – such as the number of new leads generated or sales achieved – to assess the results of a current project. You could also compare data related to your current activities to data collected over a similar time period for previous assignments.

To create a reporting system, the final step is to structure your report formats effectively. You should use a template that presents the information in an easy-to-understand way. Be sure to include all key areas of concern in your reports. And – unless they include highly sensitive information – ensure your reports are easily accessible.

Don't overload your reports, as this can make them difficult to analyze. Try to group related factors together. Items to be compared – such as projected revenues, cash flows, and costs – should be presented close to one another so that comparisons can be made easily.

If necessary, provide any percentages or ratios that are important, such as the rate of return on an investment or the profit margin – readers shouldn't have to make basic calculations themselves. And provide space in your reports for managers to note any actions they need to take, based on the information you've provided.

Question

Consider your own situation for a moment. How effective is the reporting system you currently use?

Options:

1. Extremely effective
2. Reasonably effective
3. Not very effective

Answer

Option 1: That's great! You indicate that your own reporting system is extremely effective. This means you're able to measure and assess your performance results effectively and take corrective actions when necessary.

Option 2: You're on the right track. You say your own reporting system is reasonably effective. You should look at ways of improving it, in order to improve the quality of the reports you generate.

Option 3: You indicate that your own reporting system isn't very effective. You should address this problem urgently. If you want to implement your business plans effectively, it's important to have a sound reporting system in place.

Developing control procedures

Effective implementation of your business plan involves more than reporting information in a well-designed format. You also need to put a system in place so you can use your reports for control

purposes. To develop effective reporting and control procedures, you need to decide whom to involve in your reports. Also, determine the frequency of your reports and establish a suitable performance review process.

To develop effective control procedures, you need to decide whom to involve in your reports. So first identify to whom in your organization you should distribute reports. This might be just a few key people or the entire project team.

For example, you could decide to e-mail a copy of your report to all team leaders and functional managers involved with your project. Alternatively, you might decide to distribute your report to senior executives only.

At this stage, it's important to identify the people who will be involved in deciding what actions to take next, based on the information contained in your reports. Ensure their names are on your distribution list.

Question

You should always generate a detailed management report at least once a week.

Do you think this statement is true or false?
Options:
1. True
2. False

Answer

Option 1: The statement isn't true. The frequency that you generate reports should be appropriate to the needs of your organization – and the project itself. It's not always necessary to generate weekly reports. A monthly or quarterly report might be sufficient.

Option 2: The statement is false. A weekly management report isn't always required. The frequency of reports should depend on the type of performance indicators you've chosen and on the amount of management control that needs to be exerted over specific activities in your action plan.

To develop effective control procedures, you need to decide how frequently reports should be distributed. This usually depends on the type of performance indicators you've chosen. It can also depend on the amount of management control that needs to be exerted over specific activities in your business plan.

The frequency that you deliver reports should be appropriate to the needs of your organization. For example, it's probably unnecessary to generate a daily financial report. However, a quarterly financial report might be essential.

Reports should always be produced in a timely way. For example, you won't be able to speed up the collection of outstanding payments in May if a report on the matter isn't received until June.

When developing control procedures, you also need to establish a suitable performance review process. To do this, decide whether performance review and analysis is an individual or a group activity. In other words, decide whether it's the responsibility of individual managers or the entire management team. Then you can design a review process involving the relevant individuals or groups.

Question

Imagine you're a manager in a company that designs and sells software products. You're trying to implement a business plan that aims to increase sales.

How can you create an effective reporting system to help you implement your plan?

Options:

1. Identify the number of new leads generated as a key indicator and state that 20 must be identified weekly

2. Tell the team that anyone who exceeds the new sales target will receive a bonus at the end of the year

3. Use benchmarks from other organizations to assess your own sales results to date

4. Use a template to structure your performance reports and ensure you've carried out any necessary calculations

5. Include as much data as possible in your reports, even if the data doesn't need to be analyzed by other managers

6. Avoid linking specific rewards to the achievement of performance targets, as targets are likely to change

Answer

Option 1: This option is correct. To create a reporting system, you first need to define key performance measurement areas, or indicators, in your organization.

Then you need to establish an acceptable level of performance for each indicator.

Option 2: This option is correct. It's important to relate performance measures to actual employee behavior. It's a good idea to offer employees rewards and recognition when they've achieved performance targets.

Option 3: This option is correct. When creating a reporting system, you should use comparative data to identify significant trends and relationships. This can help you assess the current performance of your employees.

Option 4: This option is correct. You should use a template that presents the information in an easy-to-understand way. You should also provide any percentages or ratios that are important, so people don't have to make basic computations themselves.

Option 5: This option is incorrect. You should avoid overloading your reports, as this can make them difficult to analyze. The information you present should be easy to read.

Option 6: This option is incorrect. Linking rewards to achievement can help you get the results you desire from your team members. It can also inspire and motivate them to continue doing excellent work.

Modifying plans

Despite the best planning and preparation, your business plan can go off track. It's important to react quickly and decisively in this situation by modifying your original plans and taking the necessary corrective action.

Next, you'll observe an interaction involving Ameera, a manager in a software company, and her boss, Leroy. Ameera is implementing a business plan to introduce a new product – but things aren't running smoothly. She needs to communicate the situation to Leroy.

Follow along as Ameera and Leroy discuss the problems she's encountered.

Ameera: So here's the deal...the new product won't be ready until end of June. Five weeks behind schedule...

Ameera is worried.

Leroy: What?! How'd you get so far behind?

Leroy is surprised.

Ameera: Turns out I was wrong. Seven programmers aren't enough. I didn't even realize how far behind I was until I printed the monthly report this morning.

Ameera is concerned.

Leroy: So you've really got two problems. You underestimated the resources. And you're not getting control reports often enough.

Leroy is calm.

Ameera: Well, I've made some changes. I'll be getting weekly reports from now on.

Ameera is positive.

Leroy: Would it help if I moved some more programmers onto your team?

Leroy is determined.

Ameera: That'd be huge! I'll start changing the schedule right away.

Ameera is pleased.

Leroy: Good. And don't forget to keep a close eye on the new control reports.

Leroy is cautious.

Ameera has to deal with a major problem – her project is five weeks behind schedule. This is because at the beginning of the project, she underestimated the resources she'd need. In addition, her reporting system is inadequate, because it should have alerted her to this problem earlier.

After her meeting with Leroy, Ameera revises her original plans to deal with the situation. She adds extra resources to her team and reschedules the entire project. She also generates control reports weekly, instead of monthly, so she's alerted to problems as early as possible.

Ameera needs to monitor the results of her revised plans closely, to ensure the project gets back on track – and stays on track. If future problems arise, she may need to modify her plans again.

Plan-modification process

The environment your organization operates in is likely to evolve over time. This makes developing a business plan an uncertain process. For instance, legislative changes or other external developments might impact your original plans. Internal developments, such as losing a key employee to a competitor, might also have to be factored in. So when implementing a business plan, you need to have clear procedures in place for modifying your action plans and strategies when necessary.

Reflect

What steps do you think you should take to modify an action plan?

Write down your response or enter it in a text file in your word-processor application (or in a text editor such as Notepad) and save it to your hard drive for later viewing.

You may have noted any of several steps to modify an action plan. The first thing you need to do is identify the problem areas in your original plan. Next, you should pinpoint the probable cause of each problem. After that, you can develop a corrective-action strategy to deal with the situation. Finally, it's important to implement and monitor the corrective strategy and the revised plan.

See each step in order to learn more about it.

1. Identify problem areas

The first step is to work out which parts of your action plan are causing you problems. In other words, you need to identify any areas of your plan where performance is below expectation.

For example, the problem may be that you're not reaching your sales targets – or the number of customer complaints may have risen.

2. Pinpoint cause of each problem

When you've identified the problems you're encountering, you need to analyze your project carefully and find out why each problem exists. At this stage, it's important to identify the root causes of problems, not the symptoms.

For example, the problem may be that you underestimated the resources you need – or perhaps you scheduled your resources incorrectly.

3. Develop corrective-action strategy

After you've pinpointed the cause of each problem, decide what actions to take to improve performance in each area. You also need to assign responsibility for each action to a particular person, to ensure it gets done.

Corrective actions might include rescheduling a project, adding more resources to a project, or redesigning a process or product.

4. Implement and monitor revised plan

The final step is to implement your revised plan. You need to know how and when the new strategies will be carried out, and by whom. Work out how you're going to monitor the revised plan, to ensure that performance improves.

For example, you could decide to generate management reports more frequently, or to generate more specific reports on problematic areas.

Being able to revise and modify your action plans when necessary is an important skill. In fact, it could be the difference between a plan failing or succeeding. So ensure you give the plan-modification process the same time and attention that you gave to the initial creation of the action plan.

When implementing a business plan, the final step you need to take is to assess the outcomes of your plan. To do this, you should evaluate the results of the planning, implementation, and control activities you've engaged in. The main aim of this evaluation is to provide you with information that will be useful in developing new business plans and strategies in the future.

Question

Match each example to the component of a plan-modification process it corresponds to.

Options:

A. The project schedule isn't being adhered to

B. The time it takes to complete each task has been miscalculated

C. Extend the deadline by one month and reschedule tasks accordingly

D. Request that a daily progress report on problematic areas be delivered to you

Targets:
1. Identify problem areas
2. Pinpoint cause of each problem
3. Develop corrective-action strategy
4. Implement and monitor revised plan

Answer

A project schedule that isn't being adhered to is an example of a problem area. You should also identify any other areas of your plan where performance is below expectation.

If the time it takes to complete each task has been miscalculated, it's likely to be the cause of at least some of the problems you've identified. Discover the cause of other problems by analyzing your project carefully.

By stating that a deadline should be extended by one month and tasks rescheduled accordingly, you're developing a corrective-action strategy. Make sure you assign responsibility for each action to a particular person.

Requesting a daily progress report on problematic areas is one way of ensuring you implement and monitor your revised plan effectively. You need to monitor the revised plan to ensure performance improves.

CHAPTER FOUR
References and glossary

References
1. *Guide to Business Planning* - 2009, Graham Friend and Stefan Zehle, Profile Books
2. *Strategic Business Planning: A Dynamic System for Improving Performance and Competitive Advantage* - 2002, Clive Reading, Kogan Page
3. *Business Planning and Control: Integrating Accounting, Strategy and People* - 2008, Bruce Bowhill, John Wiley & Sons
4. *Guide to Business Planning* - 2009, Graham Friend and Stefan Zehle, Profile Books
5. *Strategic Planning for Public and Nonprofit Organizations: A Guide to Strengthening and Sustaining Organizational Achievement, Third Edition* - 2004, John M. Bryson, Jossey-Bass
6. *How To Write A Business Plan, Fourth Edition* - 1995, Edwin T. Crego, Jr., Peter D. Schiffrin and James C. Kauss, American Management Association

7. *The Business of Government: Strategy, Implementation & Results* - 2000, Thomas G. Kessler and Patricia Kelley, Management Concepts
8. *Five Principles of Corporate Performance Management* - 2007, Bob Paladino, John Wiley & Sons

Glossary

A

action plan - A series of tasks that need to be completed in order to accomplish a particular objective.

B

benchmarking - An analysis of competitor strengths and weaknesses typically used to evaluate an organization's relative competitive position and potential improvement opportunities, and to measure success based on accepted industry best practices.

business plan - A formal plan describing business ideas and goals, with the purpose of attracting organizational approval.

business strategy - How an organization competes in a particular market. It involves making strategic decisions about products, meeting customer expectations, developing competitive advantages, and exploiting or creating new opportunities.

C

capability - Ability of an organization or business unit to reach key objectives, usually tied to core organizational objectives or mission.

contingencies - The section of the business plan where potential problems or challenges are described and solutions are suggested.

contingency plan - A coordinated set of steps to be taken to mitigate problems that occur when a business plan is implemented.

corporate strategy - The high-level scope and direction of an organization and the way in which its operations, such as business units and divisions, collaborate to help meet established goals or objectives.

E

execution - The element of a business plan that describes the development of a product or service as well as the resources needed to bring it to market.

executive summary - The abstract of the business plan, listing everything detailed in subsequent parts of the plan. It describes the organization, the business venture, product, or service and its purpose, management, operations, marketing, and finances.

external analysis - An analysis of customers, competitors, and the market.

G

gap analysis - An analysis of the difference between an organization or department's current state and its desired one.

I

implementation - The how-to section of the business plan detailing steps taken in the areas of marketing, operations and finances, and personnel.

K

key performance indicators - A group of metrics used to determine if an organization is reaching operational and performance-related goals. Indicators are often both financial and nonfinancial, and almost every organization uses a unique mix – there is no set list. These indicators also tend to be permanent and uniformly applied across the organization.

M

market opportunity - The section of the business plan that describes the needs or wants a product or service will satisfy and presents evidence of consumer demand for the product or service.

O

opportunity - The element of a business plan that describes the problem the plan will solve.

outcomes - The predicted results if a business plan is followed.

R

resource - In the context of a business plan, these are people, assets, IT, and distribution. These must be assessed when preparing to develop a business plan.

resource allocation - The process of distributing resources among business units and divisions, which often demands making strategic choices based on the typically high number of requests for funding of corporate, business, and functional programs outlined in the strategic planning process.

S

situation analysis - An analysis that considers factors within a business department or organization.

solution - The element of the business plan that describes how the problem will be solved by a particular product or service.

strategic planning process - The process of setting an organization's long-term objectives and goals, and then identifying the most effective approach for achieving them.

www.ingramcontent.com/pod-product-compliance
Lightning Source LLC
Chambersburg PA
CBHW020919180526
45163CB00007B/2802